POWER SOURCE

PARENTING

Growing Up Strong & Raising Healthy Kids

by **Bethany Casarjian**

LIONHEART PRESS

Power Source Parenting: Growing Up Strong and Raising Healthy Kids

Text copyright © 2008 by Bethany Casarjian
Illustrations copyright © 2008 by Jan Gerardi

The Lionheart Foundation
P.O. Box 194 Back Bay
Boston, MA 02117

www.lionheart.org

Printed in the United States of America

ISBN: 978-0-9799338-0-6
Library of Congress Catalog Card Number:

Book design by Cathy Bobak
Book illustration by Jan Gerardi

First edition, 2008
1 2 3 4 5 6 7 8 9 10

The Lionheart Foundation wishes to acknowledge
The Hay Foundation for the very generous donation
of the first printing of *Power Source Parenting*.

The Lionheart Foundation would like to thank the many young parents
who made this book possible. In particular we would like to
acknowledge the enormous contribution of the young mothers
at ROCA (Chelsea, MA) who participated in the
parenting journal project.

We would also like to acknowledge the young mothers at
St. Mary's Women and Children's Center (Dorchester, MA)
who helped us by sharing their voices in our parenting groups.

We also thank the young fathers who contributed
their thoughts and ideas to *Power Source Parenting*.

Contents

Introduction...I

1   Pregnant. No Way! (Yes, Way.)............................... 5

2   Being a Kid and Having a Kid................................. 11

3   So Who Are You, Really?....................................23

4   Making a Tight Bond...40

5   Coping with the Stress of Parenting in Healthy Ways......52

6   Letting Go of Negative Feelings Toward Your Child......... 68

7   The Relationship with Your Baby's Dad or Mom...........80

8   Just for Dads...114

9   Full House—Raising a Baby with Your Family.............. 121

10   Hey Grandma (or Grandpa), This One's for You............ 141

11   Helping Your Child Handle Feelings......................... 152

12   Healthy Discipline..176

13   Breaking the Cycle...222

14   The Future...248

    Bibliography..262

Introduction

I can't say that my childhood was happy. My parents were always fighting with each other and screaming at us kids. I remember being young and just wanting someone to care about me and show me some attention and love. When I found out I was pregnant, I made a promise to raise my baby different. I want her to grow up without the hurt and anger that I carried around with me. The problem is that being a parent is harder than I thought and I don't always know what to do.

Charlene, 16 years old

Who Is This Book For?

This book is written for any teenager or young person who is trying to raise a child the best way he or she can. And as you probably already know, that's a huge job. Being a parent isn't easy. In fact, ask most people and they'll tell you that it's the hardest job there is. But it can be even tougher if you are young, a single parent, struggling to find a decent job, still trying to finish school, or feel stuck in an unhealthy relationship.

Parenting can also be a big challenge if you've grown up around parents or caregivers who hurt you physically or emotionally, neglected you, or acted in other ways that caused you pain. If this happened to you, it may be hard to figure out how to be an effective parent. For the most part, we learn what we see. Even if we *want* to parent without yelling or hitting, sometimes it helps to be *shown* another way. That's where this book comes in—by answering some of those big questions and giving you some ideas about how to be a truly effective parent.

To learn more about the issues facing young parents, I asked a group of young moms and dads to meet with me every week for three months. The stories you'll read in this book are from journals they kept describing their experiences as young parents. As we spent time together, I noticed that one question kept coming up. It was, "How do I give my child something I never had?" What was the "something" they were talking about? For some girls it was love, acceptance, and support. For others it was guidance and healthy discipline. For a few it was having a mother who could keep her children safe and protected. Basically, what the mothers in our group all wanted to know was, How do I raise my child so that he or she doesn't feel the fear, disappointment, or pain that I did? And that's what this book is all about. Or maybe you had a pretty easy childhood, but find yourself with a lot of questions about how to raise your own child. This book is for you, too.

This book is also about helping you grow as a person, while finding those things already within you that will make you a nurturing, strong, and wise parent. Maybe you didn't plan on becoming a parent so young. Or maybe you wanted a child, but didn't know quite how hard it would be. No matter how you got here, learning to be an effective parent is your supreme task. It's your mission.

What's All This "Effective Parent" Stuff?

In this book we've decided to use the word effective parent instead of good parent. Why? Because sometimes people confuse being a "good parent" with being a "good person." You're all good people. But parenting is like any other skill. You have to learn it to do it well. Parenting doesn't always come naturally. And it's not like babies come with instruction manuals.

So how do we learn to become effective parents? We learn by watching other effective parents. We learn by reading books, through a visiting nurse, or by going to parenting classes. Unfortunately, there's not always someone around to show us the ropes—that's what this book is for.

The most important reason to become an effective parent is because it will save you a lot of headaches and heartaches. Effective parents usually have kids who are easier to manage, have fewer behavior problems at home and school, and end up getting involved in fewer high-risk behaviors (like drugs, crime, and violence). Now, this isn't to say that if your child is having behavior difficulties, it's all your fault and that you're a bad parent. But making a few changes in your parenting can really improve your child's behavior and give you greater peace of mind.

(And in case you're wondering, I have three little kids myself, so I know how tough parenting can be. Hopefully I can share some of what I've learned as a psychologist and a mother to make your job a little easier. Also, I work with a lot of other great people who've helped me write this book. We might not have all the answers, but we've got a lot of them!)

Power Source

Before *Power Source Parenting*, we wrote a book called *Power Source: Taking Charge of Your Life.* It's filled with stories written by young people who have gotten involved in high-risk behavior. Many come from families where there are problems like domestic violence, substance abuse, neglect, or a parent in prison. But the one thing they have in common is the desire for a better, happier life. If you haven't read *Power Source*, we encourage you to ask a counselor or teacher to contact the Lionheart Foundation to receive a copy. Thousands of kids across the country have read *Power Source* and love it. Many say it's the first book they've read that's real and has anything to do with their lives. *Power Source* puts you on the road to handling some of life's most difficult challenges, like dealing with anger or abuse. It gives you the tools to take control of your life so you don't give your power away over and over. But most importantly, *Power Source* helps you discover who you really are and the kind of future you want to have.

Chapter 1

Pregnant. No Way! (Yes, Way.)

My mother's first reaction was like, "No, not my lil' girl." All she could do was cry and cry and cry. I felt like she was ashamed of me. I was ashamed of me. And I thought she would definitely kick me out of the house 'cuz she's one of those 'you made your bed you sleep in it' types of people. But she didn't throw me out. She let me stay. After a while she was okay about it even though she thinks I messed up my life. Me? I felt stupid, like how could I do that to myself. At first I was in shock and just didn't believe it. When it finally sunk in I just sat around the house wondering, "So how's this gonna work?"

Charlene, 16 years old

I'm Pregnant... Now What?

Welcome to the shortest chapter in the book. Actually, it makes sense that it's the shortest chapter, because pregnancy is the shortest part of being a parent. Think about it. Pregnancy lasts for nine months, but if you choose to become a parent, you'll be one for the rest of your life.

The other reason this is a short chapter is because this book is not about your decision whether or not to become a parent. There are other options out there. Only you (and people who have your very best interests at heart) can make that decision. And we know how hard that choice is to make. Take the time you need. Listen to your gut. Talk to other people who have been through it and really listen to what they have to say. Be as honest (and gentle) with yourself as possible, and chances are you'll make the right choice.

Dealing with the Feelings

When you first find out you're pregnant, you might have a lot of different feelings. There's no one way for people to react. However, many teens describe feeling shock and denial at first, like it couldn't really be true. Most people feel like it couldn't happen to them. Then other feelings wash over them, like fear, worry, regret, shame, and anger. These are all natural and they don't last forever. Know that you're not alone. When most young people find out they're pregnant, they feel the same way. If you can, talk to other people who have some wisdom about the whole thing. We're not saying that you need to tell everyone on the street your business, but keeping your pregnancy a secret can make everything seem worse and cause painful feelings to build up. Even finding one trusted person you can confide in can release some of the pressure and fear you might be feeling.

Other Peoples' Reactions

The first person I told when I found out I was pregnant was my boyfriend. He totally flipped out because he didn't want a baby and he told me to have an abortion, but I didn't want an abortion. So I decided to keep the baby and he broke up with me. That hurt because I thought he really cared for me. So I went through most of my pregnancy alone and right before I was supposed to have the baby he came back around. Then he started touching my stomach and he told everyone about the baby and people were happy for him. Things started changing between us and he was nicer to me. We're still together. I'm glad I didn't have the abortion just to hold onto a guy, 'cuz I really don't think that'll work. I made the right choice for me.

Carrie, 17 years old

No matter what choice you make, you'll have to deal with other peoples' reactions to your pregnancy: parents, boyfriends, friends, teachers, neighbors, sometimes even the doctors you see. Lots of people will have an opinion about what you should do. Some people might even be openly judgmental.

I saw the neighbors looking at me and shaking their heads and I heard the gossip going around. But the thing that hurt me the most is when my father and me got into a fight and he called me a whore. When he said that it made me feel like I was the worst person in the world. I know it's not true, but it's hard to take coming from your father.

Latisha, 17 years old

People's negative reactions can make feelings like shame, embarrassment, fear, sadness, and confusion even stronger. While people's first responses to your pregnancy can be hard to bear, it's important to remember that they often change over time. People might think, "Oh, she's too young and irresponsible to take care of a baby." But you can prove them wrong by stepping up to the plate. You often can't control or change how people respond to your pregnancy. But you can sometimes gain their respect by becoming an effective and reliable parent.

Unfortunately, some people might hold on to their judgment or doubt about you even if you are a responsible and dedicated parent. Remind yourself not to get caught up in their negativity. No matter what other people think, don't lose sight of the fact that you are still a strong, wise, good person. Even if you messed up and got pregnant by accident, that doesn't change the power and goodness in you. Holding on to that truth can sometimes make it easier to deal with the world around us.

Making the Promise

When I got pregnant it was cool and fun. People like my mother and boyfriend spoiled me and got me whatever I wanted. They was always asking me how I felt and could I get you something to eat. Everyone in school wanted to ask me questions about being pregnant. I felt special and important. But now the baby's here and it's like night and day. Everyone is worrying about the baby and they're giving no thoughts to how I feel. I love the baby and all. I mean, he's my life, but it's like no one cares about how I'm doing anymore.

Diamond, 18 years old

Like we said, there's a big difference between nine months of pregnancy and twenty (or more) years of raising a child. Pregnancy is mostly about you. It's exciting. People might take care of you. You're the center of attention. Not so once you become a parent. Parenting isn't really about your needs, it's about the baby's needs. It's not about your comfort as much as the baby's. Mostly, it's about giving, not about getting. Of course, you have to take care of yourself in order to be a good parent. But a lot of times, being a parent means giving things up for the sake of your child.

To really get the job of parenting done right, you have to make a promise. It's a promise to get up every morning and do the best job you can. We know that nobody's perfect. We all make mistakes. But day in and day out, the job of parenting requires that you do what's right instead of what's easy. Being a parent asks you to take this job to heart and bring your whole self to it every single day. Sounds tough, but in the long run there's a huge payoff. By making sacrifices, both big and small, you raise the healthiest baby you can. This is the promise we ask you to make to yourself and your child as you read this book.

Chapter 2

Being a Kid and Having a Kid

In most ways I feel too young to have a baby. I'm also scared because I don't know what kind of father my boyfriend is gonna be. I'm gonna have to quit all the stuff I been doing like hanging out all day with my friends just smokin' and chillin'. Now I'm gonna have to make decisions for two people, not just me. Also I'm afraid about how we're gonna support this baby. It's coming in two months and my boyfriend don't have no job. We have no crib, no car seat, no stroller, no nothing. I know it's all gonna work out. Sometimes I just feel like it's a lot to deal with for a teenager.

Sandra, 15 years old

When my girl told me she was pregnant, I was like, oh shit. I didn't plan on having no baby when I was 16 years old. I wanted to be hanging with my boys, partying, you know. Doing what young people do. When she was pregnant I wasn't really there for her. I could see my whole life flash before my eyes. And that scared me. I just wasn't ready to give up my freedom. But once you have a baby, you can't be the kid no more. You need to be a man.

Marcus, 17 years old

Life Goes On

Becoming a teenage parent doesn't mean your life has ended. But as you probably already know, everything changes big-time. Having a baby changes every parent's life. But the shake-up of becoming a parent is even bigger if you're a teenager. Here are some of the ways your life is likely to change.

BEFORE the Baby	AFTER the Baby
Not so much responsibility	Lots of responsibility
Freedom to do what you want	Very little freedom
No schedule—do what you want when you want	Have to be on the baby's schedule
Hang out with friends a lot	Stay at home more
Lots of free time	Not so much free time
Spend money on yourself	Spend most of your money on the baby
Make choices that are right for just you	Have to think about what's right for the baby
Lots of time for you and boyfriend/girlfriend to hang out	Parents spend time taking care of baby—less time for the relationship

Dealing with the Responsibility

Before I got pregnant my responsibilities were to take a shower and clean my room (which I never did). Believe it or not my mother did everything for me. She washed my dishes and my clothes. She did all the shopping and cooking. I did nothing but chill with my friends and go to school. So when I had the baby it was real hard on me. I moved in with my boyfriend and it was all on me. I couldn't even fry an egg. It was a big hit on the head learning everything at once. I knew nothing about money either. But now I learned how to budget out my money for diapers and other stuff for the baby and if there's money left over, then things for me. It's good now, because I learned everything in half the time that most of my friends did. But for a while it was scary.

Erica, 19 years old

It can be scary to know that a human being's life depends on you, especially if you aren't used to having so much responsibility on your shoulders. Some of the kids we talk to say it's like having a giant weight on their backs. No wonder. Going from zero responsibility to a lot is pretty hard core. But you can do it. Taking one step at a time can help. Learn what you have to know in order to take care of the baby for that day or week.

In our young mothers' group, one young woman was worried about all the mistakes she had made in her past and how her daughter would probably end up getting tattoos all over her body like she had. She started worrying about her baby's future and getting upset. Just then, the baby made a loud sound letting everyone know that she needed a diaper change. Another girl in the group had good advice. She said, "I can't do nothing about the tattoos she might get when she's a teenager. But I have a diaper in my bag if you need to change her."

Sounds funny, but it makes sense. Don't worry about things that you don't have to worry about. Planning is good, but just do the best job you can right now. When the responsibility seems overwhelming:

STOP. BREATHE.
AND REMIND YOURSELF TO
TAKE ONE DAY AT A TIME.

Missing Out

Once I got pregnant, things really changed with my friends. Maybe they thought I was slowing them down. They couldn't smoke in the car or around me. I stopped drinking so I couldn't party with them anymore. It's not that they didn't want to be there for me, but I just wasn't as much fun for them to hang around with. Also they got pissed off because they thought teachers let me get away with a lot at school because I was pregnant. Everyone was treating me different. They never called me to go to clubs because they thought that my big belly would chase guys away. Their families told them not to hang out with me because I was a bad influence. Once the baby came, things got even worse.

I couldn't go out ever because I couldn't find a sitter. Then they almost never came around.

Lisa, 18 years old

One of the hardest things to deal with about becoming a teenage parent is feeling like you're missing out on the best parts of being young—hanging out with friends, having fun, being free. If you have a baby, you know that it's almost impossible to do those things like you used to. And that can be a hard pill to swallow. Lots of things get in the way, like finding someone to watch the baby. If your mom is helping you take care of your child, she might feel resentful if you are going out to hang out with friends. She might feel that it's your responsibility to stay home and take care of your child. You probably have less money to spend when you go out than before you had a baby. Babies take a lot of money to raise. And most people taking care of children all day are sometimes too tired to even think of going out.

As honestly as you can, write down some of the things you are missing out on by having a baby.

_____

_____

_____

_____

_____

_____

Now take some time to write down how missing out makes you feel.

_____

_____

_____

_____

_____

Not going out can make you feel like you're missing out and can even lead to feelings of resentment toward the baby. All parents need to hang out with people their own age. Especially young parents. You probably won't go out as much and do all the things you did before you had the baby. But it's important not to isolate yourself from other people your age. Being with friends is important. It's a chance to connect and refuel and have a little fun. So what can you do about it? Here a few ideas that other young parents have tried.

Ways to Stay Connected to Friends and Have Fun

- See if you can find activities your friends are into that you can take the baby along for, like going to a park or the mall for a short time. (But be realistic. If you have an active two-year-old, the mall might not be a good choice. He'll want to run around and you might just be chasing him rather than hanging with friends.)

- Explain to your mother that you understand what your responsibilities are, but that you'd really appreciate it if she could watch the baby for just two or three hours a week so you could go out. (Find something cheap to do if you do go out so you're not broke for the next week.)

• Swap babysitting with a friend. You watch her child for three hours one week, she'll pay you back the next week. Pick someone you can trust so the baby is safe. Make sure the street goes two ways so you don't get walked on— doing all the sitting and getting nothing back.

• If the baby's father is also a caretaker, work it out with him so that a few hours a week you get to get out and enjoy yourself and give him the same opportunity.

Giving Up on Going Out

I want to hang with my friends and go to parties and have fun, but with a baby you can't really do any of those things. Now everything is about the baby. My life has changed a lot. Now it's baby this and baby that. The responsibility and the missing out feel hard. You got to make sure he's got his food and that he's okay. When my friends call up I feel this pull in my stomach to go with them. Then I look at my baby and realize I can't. It sounds like I'm complaining, but I'm not. I made my choice and I love my baby. Still, sometimes it's hard to sit at home knowing they're out having a good time.

Gina, 17 years old

There might be times when you're dying to get a break or go along with friends, but no one is there to cover for you and you just can't bring the baby. These are the times it might really feel like you're trapped or missing out. These are the times that you might even regret having a baby. But there are some ways to look at the situation that can bring you peace and remind you of your mission.

Having young children who need you all the time won't last forever, even if it feels like it. Little kids grow up fast, and at some point you'll have more time for yourself.

Every sacrifice you make is worth it. Doing right by your baby sometimes means you sacrifice something you want. And missing out on something you want for the sake of your baby is a wise and mature action. It's your gift to her. Give yourself credit for doing it!

Make New Friends

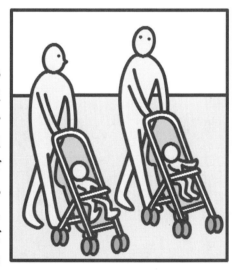

After Amara had her first baby, she was sure that she had made the biggest mistake of her life. She had met her boyfriend in drug treatment and neither of them was really ready to have a baby. After the baby was born, they moved into the top floor of his parents' house. Everyone else in the family worked, so all day long Amara was left home with a colicky, screaming baby. She had no friends because the treatment center was in the town where her boyfriend grew up, but across the country from where she was raised. Deep in her heart she was afraid that the stress was going to push her to start using again.

One day she thought she would go crazy from sitting alone in the house. It was kind of a cold winter day, but she bundled herself and the baby up in warm clothes and went out to the park. She put the baby in the swing and pushed her. Pretty soon another young woman came up with a baby who looked the same age as Amara's baby. Amara was so lonely that she just started talking to this other girl about everything that was going on in her life. The girl was cool and said that she could relate because she felt the same way a lot of time. Soon they were hanging out with each other in the mornings and the babies would play on the floor with some toys. Amara felt like a dark cloud had been lifted from her life.

If you don't have your old friends to hang with anymore, make new ones. More importantly, make new ones who have kids! Talking to other people going through the same things you are is important. They know the deal. They can relate. Plus, you'll be able to hang out together and do things that your kids can do. Rather than going clubbing, you can hang out at the park. Instead of partying, you can bust open some Play Doh. If this sounds lame or like a letdown, remember, it beats being alone.

I don't know what I would do if I didn't have Jackie (my best friend). I met her at a parenting group and we've hung out ever since. Before that I didn't really have no one. She really gets what I'm going through with my baby and my baby daddy. We chill when we ain't working or going to school. † helps me a lot just to know that I have someone who understands me.

Shana, 16 years old

When Others Treat You Like a Kid

Even if you have been through a lot in your life or taken care of brothers and sisters, the world might see you as just a kid. Part of you might feel like having a kid means you should be treated like an adult. It makes sense. You have all this responsibility. You've given up a lot that goes along with being a kid. Unfortunately, that respect doesn't always come right away. Doctors might talk down to you, and your parents might chip away at your authority with your child.

> My son got sick last week and it really stressed me out. But what stressed me out more was the way they treated me at the hospital. The doctor acted like I was lying to him or just stupid. And that really bothers me because even though I'm young, I know how to take care of my baby. I'm doing this by myself and I'm doin' a damn good job. So please don't treat me like I'm some ignorant little kid. It really bothered me when the doctor and the nurses treated me that way.
>
> Angela, 17 years old

When people treat you in a way that is disrespectful of your ability to be an effective parent, it can be hard. It might bring up feelings of embarrassment, insecurity, and doubt about whether you can do the job. Keep in mind, there's no age limit to being an effective parent. Someone who's twice your age might be a really ineffective parent. Being an effective parent isn't about your age. What being an effective parent boils down to is an openness to learning, a willingness to listen to others, not giving up, being connected to your baby, and trusting your gut.

Where to GET HELP

Look around you. Ask yourself, "What kind of parent do I want to be?" As parents, we all benefit from the wisdom of mothers who have been through it before and know the ropes. Maybe it's not your mother who you want to guide you, but an aunt, grandmother, a nurse who's been helping you with the baby, or someone in your neighborhood who you think is an effective and loving parent. Most of what parents know, they learned from watching someone else. Your job is to find the best role model you can. And when it comes to finding a parenting role model, trust your gut!

Sometimes we look around at our families and friends and don't find anyone willing or able to help us. Don't give up. There are places out there where you can find help. Below we've listed just a few ideas of where you can turn if you find yourself on your own and in need of help.

- **Parenting programs** in the hospital where you gave birth. Or ask your child's pediatrician if she or he can connect you with a visiting nurse program. There are also lactation consultants who can come to your house if you are having trouble nursing.

- **Church groups.** If you are connected to a church, this can be a very strong support network for you.

- **Teen groups** or teen centers in your community, like Girls and Boys Club.

Chapter 3

So Who Are You, Really?

I am a strong, independent woman. I am a student and a worker. I am a daughter, a sister, and a friend. I have screwed up a lot in my life. I am funny and brave and kind. I am a mother.

Lisa, 18 years old

A Work in Progress

A big part of being a young person is figuring out who you really are. That's a tough enough job as it is. But becoming a young parent adds a twist to it. Now you have two important jobs ahead of you. The good news is that becoming a parent can show you the best of who you are. It can help you discover a kind of wisdom, patience, maturity, and selflessness that you never knew you had. Seeing these incredible things can be proof that you have the power and strength to be and do anything you set your mind to.

In this chapter we're going to ask you to ask yourself who you really are. In doing so, we hope you start to create a vision of the person and the parent you want to be.

Who I Thought I Was P.B. (Pre-Baby, not Peanut Butter)

Before you became a parent, you might have thought of yourself as a son or daughter, a brother or sister, a student, a friend, "class clown," "bad girl," a ballplayer, a singer, or any other role you played. But is this all of who you are?

You might have strongly identified with a personality characteristic like funny, smart, a loner, loyal, or tough. Maybe you thought of yourself by your race or ethnicity: Black, Hispanic, Caucasian, Native American, West Indian, Spanish speaking, African, Middle Eastern, Puerto Rican, or anything else. Or maybe you felt like your emotions defined who you were, like angry, sad, depressed, happy, confused, or scared. But what else is there to you?

Once the baby came along, your thoughts about who you were may have changed big-time, especially if you are the primary caretaker. You may have put those other roles or identities on the back burner and said, "Now I am a parent." In fact, some people tell us that they actually had a baby to figure out who they were. And while being a parent is a huge, huge part of your life, believe it or not, who you really are is even bigger.

 **STOP AND THINK**

Ask yourself the question, "Who am I really?" Then write the answers here.

I am_____

I am_____

I am_____

I am_____

I am_____

I am_____

I am_____

The Core Self

While all of these things are a part of who you are, there's something deeper and more permanent. We call it the Core Self or the True Self. The Core Self is the deepest part of your nature. It is good, powerful, wise, creative, patient, strong, and peaceful. We are all born into the word with this Core Self. And the Core Self is who we truly are. The Core Self is permanent. That means no matter how many mistakes you make or how many times you screw up, the Core Self is still there with all of its power and goodness. Period. Nothing can destroy the Core Self. That doesn't mean that you don't have to take responsibility for your behavior. If you mess up or cause someone pain, it's on you to do the right thing and deal with it. But under the negative behavior is the strong, wise, deeper part of who you really are, willing to guide you if you are ready to listen.

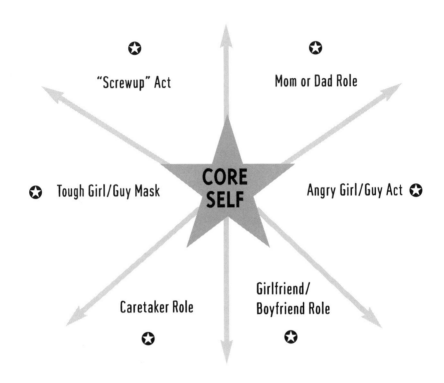

Tuning in to the Core Self

You might say, "I never feel powerful or wise." And that's because it's easy to get disconnected from our True Self, especially if we make choices that hurt us or others. But that doesn't mean that the Core Self isn't there. Or people might have treated us badly our whole lives and told us that we're stupid, no good, a loser, nothing but trouble, irresponsible, or useless. These things get into our heads and sometimes block us from connecting to our true nature.

Think of the Core Self as a radio station. You might not have the dial tuned to the right place on the radio. So all you hear is a lot of static. But that doesn't mean that the station is gone, it just means that you need to move the dial. It's the same with the Core Self. No matter how out of touch you get, it's waiting there to offer you the peace, power, strength, and wisdom that you already possess. Why is it important to tune into the Core Self? Because as long as you are listening to it, you won't be steered in the wrong direction as a person and as a parent. It is the real source of power and freedom in our lives.

I've screwed up a lot in my life and done a lot of crazy things that I wish I never did. For a long time I thought I was a bad person because of it. People always told me I was trash and I came to believe it myself. But now I know that the real me—the good me—was always there. Those things I did were just messed-up ways to get attention. Now I see there's a part of me that's stronger and bigger than my mistakes.

Erin, 19 years old

 **STOP AND THINK**

Take a moment and think back to a time when you felt connected to your Core Self and write about it. Maybe it was while being with someone you loved. Maybe it was doing the right thing. Maybe it was a time just being by yourself and feeling good.

A time I was connected to the Core Self was _____

_____

_____

_____

_____

_____

_____

_____

I felt_____

_____

_____

_____

_____

How the Core Self Helps Us Parent

The truth is, being in touch with the Core Self makes us better parents. It lets us bring the best of who we are to the job. When we are in touch with the Core Self, we aren't caught up in any act like "mad-at-the-world girl" or "hustler." We treat ourselves and our children with patience, love, and respect. That doesn't mean we won't make mistakes. We will! But being connected to the Core

Self helps us fix our parenting mistakes quicker because we aren't lost in some act or role. We might still get angry, but we don't get stuck there for days. We see that underneath the anger is peacefulness and wisdom. Being in touch with the Core Self means that we don't get lost in the storm. We become clear about what's right, safe, and wise. We become brave enough to do the thoughtful, compassionate thing for our children and ourselves.

Trust Your Gut (Listen to the Core Self)

One time I was with my girls and we wanted to go over to another friend's house across town. One of the girls had a car, but I just had my stroller and no car seat for the baby. They was like, "Jump in, nothin's gonna happen. It's just a short little ride." I knew in my heart that it was stupid, but I got in and put the baby on my lap. The girl driving just got her license and wasn't that good of a driver. Sure enough, she tried to make it through a yellow light that was turning red. We almost got hit by this truck. I started screaming at her to pull over and let us out. For the rest of the day I was mad at myself that I did that.

Jennifer, 17 years old

Do you ever have a little voice in your head that says, "Hmmmm, this doesn't feel like a good idea"? Well if you have, you're lucky. Chances are that it's your parent radar going off. Parent radar is the feeling we get when something is about to happen or is already going on that might be dangerous to our child. If your parent radar goes off, following these steps can help you make a better, safer choice.

When Your Parent Radar Goes Off...

1) Stop. Don't take another step.

2) Look at the situation carefully.

3) Think through the consequences of your choices. What might happen if you go ahead. Could anyone get hurt? Think about the worst possible outcome and ask yourself if it's worth taking the risk.

4) Make your choice. But check in again with the radar. You can always change your mind. If a situation feels unsafe to you or your baby, get out of it.

No one is too young to have parent radar. We all have it, but it takes some practice hearing it. Or if you do hear the parent radar go off, you might not be sure what to do about it. The most dangerous thing you can do is to ignore it. **Don't talk yourself out of hearing the radar.** Sometimes the radar goes off, but we don't want to listen to it because it means that we might miss out on something we want to do. This is very dangerous. By closing our ears and eyes to our parent radar, we risk placing ourselves or our babies in danger. Most of the time, when we listen to our guts, we have fewer regrets.

Calming Difficult Emotions with the Core Self

There was a few times when I was having a bad day with my boyfriend and then at work. I was freaking heated! I was so caught up in being pissed off that everything else was adding to that and making me even more pissed off. One time I was like this and I walked in the house. My daughter was acting up and I just hit her—pow, pow. Oh my God, I felt so bad. I went from mad to guilty and sad. I'm doing better about it now. When I get mad, I remember to breathe and get in touch with that calm place that is way down deep in me. Sometimes I'm so steamed that I swear it isn't there. But it is and I keep breathing and breathing until I get there.

Angela, 17 years old

Have you ever seen the ocean when there's a storm? The water gets so rough that it can destroy ships. But underneath the surface, at the bottom of the ocean's floor, it is completely calm and peaceful. It's like another world. Being in touch with the Core Self is like that. No matter what is going on around you, there is a place deep down inside of you that is peaceful. **You have the power to tap into that calm, soothing place anytime you want.** It may take practice to get there, but it's always there waiting.

When you are a parent, it is very important to tap into the Core Self as much as possible, especially when you are angry or stressed or need to make a tough choice. Listening to the wise voice of the Core Self is the first step in being an effective parent. We'll talk about ways to handle stress and anger a lot more in this book. But for right now, just know that under any stress, anger, sadness, resentment, or any other feeling parenting can cause, there is the Core Self. Always.

Seeing the Core Self of Your Child

Just as you were born into the world good, loveable, and inno-cent, so was your child. We sometimes hear people say that their child was born bad or difficult. There are children whose behavior is challenging or hard to deal with. But their true nature is goodness. And one of your biggest jobs as a parent is to see the Core Self of your child and teach him to see it, too. Next time negative thoughts creep into your mind about your child, challenge yourself to see the good, wonderful, loving core of who he really is!

Becoming a Parent, Getting Straight

Before I got pregnant I was a whole different person. I was running the streets drinking, smoking weed, and getting into trouble. Doing everything I wasn't supposed to do. I went to school but I didn't do good until the last minute and barely passed. I was constantly fighting with my mom and got kicked out of the house and had to live with friends. I went from house to house not knowing where I was going next, not knowing what was going to happen to me. I can actually say that I didn't care about myself at all. I just wanted to hang out all the time with my friends and my boyfriend and live life my way with no one telling me what to do. At the beginning of the summer I made up with my mom and one month later I was pregnant. Talk about a smack in the face. Talk about a reality check. At first I didn't know what to do. Should we keep the baby or not? Finally, my boyfriend and I decided that we would raise the baby together. I knew at that point that I had to change my life around big-time. And I did. I quit hanging out and stopped smoking and drinking cold turkey. Anything that was dangerous to me was dangerous to the baby, so I knocked that stuff off fast. I never had doubts about the kind of mother I would be. I knew that I would be a mother who put her baby first and I did. And I still do. I feel like having my son forced me to straighten out, and it's been a good thing for both of us.

Erin, 19 years old

It was bad before I had my son. I was in a gang and deep into the street life. By the time I was 18 I had been in and out of jail three times. My mom had begged me to quit because she was afraid that the same thing that happened to my brother would happen to me (Jordan's brother was shot and killed by a rival gang member). But nothing could pull me away from the cash I was pullin' in and the respect I thought I had from people on the street. When Erin told me that she was pregnant, I'm not gonna front you. I wasn't none too happy. But we talked about it and decided that we wanted to keep the baby. Down deep I knew I could be the kind of father that I never had. So I decided to straighten out and get clean from everything I had been doing. It's not always easy. I see my boys out on the street and they try to pull me back in. But I made up my mind that I'm through with all that. My son is almost two. I want him to see the kind of man who takes care of his responsibilities and isn't always running in and out of jail. My son gives me the strength to get up every day and do what I got to do—the right way.

Jordan (Erin's boyfriend), 21 years old

New Beginnings

Figuring out who we are isn't always easy. Sometimes when we're deciding who we want to be, we try things on for size. Some people get involved in gangs or high-risk behavior as a way to fit in and make an identity for themselves. Part of you might know deep down that this isn't who you really are—but it can be hard to stop this way of living, especially if you don't know what else to do. Or some people want to straighten out, but keep putting it off. "Next week I'll start going to school." "I'll just do _____ (any high-risk behavior) one more time and then I'll stop."

But becoming a parent is the perfect time to create a new identity. Becoming a parent is a chance to look at things in your life and make a choice about whether they should stay or go. And it all starts with a simple question: **What kind of person and parent do I want to be?** Use *this question* to help you decide *these kinds of questions…*

> • Which friends should I keep? Which ones will support me being a good parent?

> • How important is school to my future and my child's future?

> • What kinds of behaviors are safe and which ones do I need to stop doing (drugs, alcohol, high-risk or offending behaviors, hanging out in dangerous places, not caring for my body)?

> • What kind of environment do I want my baby to grow up in?

Everything You Need to Be a Good Parent is Already inside of You

Before I became a parent, I really didn't believe I could accomplish much. I was a terrible student. I never was good at sports or art or anything. People never seemed to believe in me, so I really did wonder what kind of parent I was going to be. But now I see a side of me that I never knew I had. I am gentle and patient and I know that I'm doing good taking care of my daughter. It's the first thing I've ever really been good at and it makes me proud.

Shana, 16 years old

True, there's no owner's manual for raising a child. And while you may need a few pointers on how to get the parenting thing in full swing, everything you need to be a good parent is already in you waiting to shine! Parenting can show us our hidden strengths. Like a person who never really spoke up for himself might find that he can be bold and assertive for his child. Or you might have thought of yourself as really impatient, but find you can be extremely patient with your child. Maybe you are still discovering these strengths about yourself. Parenting offers us plenty of chances to grow and see the truly amazing things we're capable of!

Write down five strengths you have learned about yourself since becoming a parent.

1._____

2._____

3._____

4._____

5._____

It's Not You (Being a Parent is Hard!)

Before I became a mother I wasn't as negative about myself as I am now. Now I feel very insecure and like nothing I do is right. The house is never clean, I have trouble getting everything done that I'm supposed to do. I'm having a really hard job concentrating on my schoolwork because I'm so tired. Plus, half the time I'm not sure if I'm doing things right with the baby. Should I let her sleep in my bed? Is she eating right? There are days when I just feel like giving up.

Janet, 18 years old

Parenting can make everyone doubt themselves. This can be especially true if you're a young parent. Am I old enough? Mature enough? Strong enough? Or patient enough? The answer to all of those questions is yes. But sometimes we all feel convinced that we haven't got what it takes. When you find yourself having one of those days, keep in mind that being a parent is the toughest job in the world. The more connected you are to your Core Self, the easier it is to pick yourself up after a hard day of parenting. By tuning in to the Core Self, we remind ourselves that parenting might be tough, but so are we! We might make mistakes, but we have the power to learn from them and make things better for our children.

Ways to Get in Touch with the Core Self

The more you are in touch with the Core Self, the more grounded and powerful you'll be as a person and parent. These are some ways to get connected to that power and peace.

1) Talk with someone real. Find someone you can be yourself with. Use this person to get in tune with the deepest, most genuine part of you. This is the place where wisdom and clarity are. Listen to the Core Self when you need to make decisions that take some thought.

2) Do something good, honest, right, or trustworthy. This can be something for your child or anyone else. By doing something we know in our gut is right, we tap into the heart of who we really are.

3) Exercise. Sometimes working out can quiet the "chatter" or noise in our minds so that we can hear the voice of Self again.

4) Meditate. It brings us back to the inner power and peace of the Self. (See pages 61-62 for instructions.)

5) Be in nature. No matter where you live, there's almost always a park nearby. Or if you live in a rural area, you might see nature all around you. Oftentimes we overlook the incredible power and beauty of the trees, the sky, the water, and the earth. But the power and beauty of nature is the same power and beauty inside of you.

6) Tune into Your Higher Power or God. For lots of people, praying reconnects them to their Core Self. Talk to your Higher Power. Ask for help. Listen with all your heart.

7) See Your Child's Core Self. Take a minute to go beyond your child's latest phase, behaviors, or emotions. Look deeply to the beauty, goodness, and light that is at the center of your child. The more you connect with this part of your child, the more in tune you'll be with your own Core Self.

8) Take Time to Remind Yourself:

No matter what, my core goodness can't be destroyed.

No matter what mistakes you make, the goodness of Self is forever. This is a basic truth.

Chapter 4

Making a Tight Bond

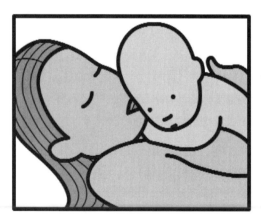

I don't want my baby to grow up being scared of the world like I was. I am going to be there for her every step of the way. When she cries, I will let her know that she's safe with her mother. When she hurts, I will comfort her. I didn't get that from my mother. Maybe that's why I always feel alone. Or maybe that's why it's so hard for me to trust people. But I'm going to do my best to make sure that my baby doesn't have those same scared and empty feelings like me.

Denise, 20 years old

The first and the most important job you have as a parent is to form a healthy bond to your child. Another word for the close connection you form to your child is "attachment." What does that mean? It means that your number one job from the minute you set eyes on your baby is to make her feel that she can trust you. Babies who can trust their caregiver believe that the world is safe. Feeling safe with their parent is absolutely necessary for babies to learn and develop in emotionally healthy ways. Think about it. Your baby comes into the world completely dependent on you. (Did you know that your baby for a long time actually thinks she's the same person as you! For real!) You're her entire world. If she's left to cry, treated roughly, not held or rocked or soothed, what is her world like? How will she feel?

Why is Bonding So important?

Babies who have strong and positive bonds to their parents

Do better in school

Make friends more easily

Have fewer behavior problems, like fighting and breaking rules

Are less likely to use drugs when they get older

Feel better about themselves

Grow up to have better relationships

The lessons she learns from you in the first few months of her life will teach her whether she can trust. And being able to trust is a big advantage in life. In these very early months, you are giving her a picture of the world that will stay in her brain for the rest of her life. If she feels loved, she will grow to feel good about herself. She will feel secure. We don't mean to scare you or freak you out, but these early months are incredibly powerful and important!

The good thing about bonding with your baby is that it's totally in your power. You don't need a degree to do it. You don't need money to do it. And you don't need any special toys or gadgets. Anyone can bond with their baby if they know what to do.

So, How Do I Make Her Trust Me?

For something that is so incredibly important, it's actually easy to do. When your baby is very young (newborn to 4 months) this means picking her up whenever she cries. It also means feeding her whenever she is hungry (whether it's convenient or not). If she is upset or uncomfortable, soothe her by rocking her gently and singing in a low, quiet voice.

Always touch your baby gently. Babies who are handled roughly learn that the world is rough. If they are treated carelessly or harshly through the first year, they will start treating the world (and all the people in it) the same way. **Even if you are very tired, stressed, or frustrated, dig deep and find the patience to treat her softly and with tenderness.**

Building Trust in the Middle of the Night

It's so hard when she wakes up in the middle of the night when I been up all day doin' this, runnin' here. I'm worn out at night and I just can't take getting up. One thing I feel bad about, though, is the *other night she woke me up right after I fell asleep. I just started screaming at her father to get up. Why am I always the one who has to get up? Then he starts yelling at me that he has to go to work in the morning and he needs his rest. All this screaming and nobody pickin' up the baby. Soon I noticed that she was screamin' harder too. Her face was all red and puffy. Then I felt bad, like I was making her feel worse instead of better.*

Janet, 18 years old

Take 1—Let's say that you had a really long day with your baby. She was cranky and whiney all day. Maybe you have other stress going on in your house or trouble with your boyfriend. All you want to do is catch some sleep. You get the baby down and then you crawl into bed. About an hour later, you hear crying. Now, here's where the trust part comes in. If you get angry, jump out of bed, pick up the baby roughly, grab a bottle, and feed her in a stressed-out way, she will pick up on that. She will not feel safe and comforted. It might even make it harder to calm her down and get her back to sleep.

We've all been there. Tired out of our minds. **You might think the baby is too young to pick up on your feelings, but she isn't.** So how do you make her feel calm when you're not?

Take 2—Picture it happening another way. . . . This time when you hear her cry, before you move a muscle, take a few deep breaths. Now you walk over to the crib and look at her. Instead of seeing a person who is keeping you from sleep, or someone who is bothering you, try and see the baby for who she really is—an innocent person who needs your help. She is no different than any baby. All babies need their mothers (or fathers) at all hours. She is not doing this on purpose. It is your job to soothe and calm her. It is your job to teach her that you will keep her safe in the world. Sure, it's hard to miss out on sleep, but this stage doesn't last long. Before you touch her, smile at her. Sounds corny, but it works. Use a calm and soothing voice when you talk. Pick her up with gentle hands. When you have calmed her, feel proud. You're awesome and your baby is lucky to have a mom or dad who can do this for her.

When She's Little, She Can't Be Spoiled

I'm not sure what to do when she cries. I don't want to pick her up all the time because my grandmother says that will spoil her. I got some people telling me to hold her. I got other people telling me to let her cry it out. I don't know what to do. Help!!!!

Stephanie, 16 years old

It can be confusing when you get a lot of different advice coming at you. But the real deal is that you can't spoil a very young baby. If your very young (0-4 months) baby is crying, she needs your help. Maybe she's hungry, tired, scared, or cold. Sometimes it's hard to figure out what's wrong. That's okay. Soothe her the best you can. Sometimes you can't make a baby stop crying. That's okay, too. The most important thing you can do is to show her that she is safe and cared for. And remember, no amount of love and affection will spoil any baby.

If your baby is older, like from 5 months and up, take a minute and listen to his cry. You've probably figured out that babies have different cries for pain, hunger, boredom and frustration. If a seven-month-old baby is frustrated, you might wait a second before rushing into the living room to help him. Maybe he'll work it out on his own. If he does, give him lots of praise. If a nine-month-old is hungry and crying, explain to her that food is on the way. Let her know that you understand what she needs—even if she can't have it right away. Tune in to your baby and let them know you "get" what they're feeling. This isn't spoiling. It's part of building trust.

Easy Babies Still Need You

When babies cry a lot or are fussy, it's like an alarm. They are always reminding us to take care of them. But don't forget that quiet, easy babies need lots of touch time too. It's easy to be tempted to put an easy baby in a stroller for hours at a time—especially if he seems happy. Don't park your baby in a place where he's getting no stimulation or contact from people (unless he's sleeping or overtired). All babies need to be held and touched. It is required for them to grow. Carrying babies in a snuggly or other carriers you wear on your chest is a great way for the baby to be in contact with you. And it still lets you walk around and do other things.

Building Trust with Older Babies

Older babies are also learning about trust from you. Starting when he's about six to eight months old, your baby might suddenly become afraid of strangers. Maybe when he was four months old he loved to be rocked by people he didn't know, but now he screams bloody murder if strangers even look at him. This is normal and is called stranger anxiety. (All babies have stranger anxiety. And it's healthy.) He might even get upset if people he knows (but doesn't see too much) try to get close to him. By the age of 18 months, this stage will be over. But he needs you to help him through it. To build trust with your older baby, you need to make him feel safe and reduce his stress and anxiety. Don't ignore his fear or act like he's "doing it on purpose." Instead, try this. . .

Dealing with Stranger Anxiety

• Remind yourself that stranger anxiety is normal and healthy.

• Respecting his fear is not spoiling him!

• Help your baby feel safe by holding him and talking gently.

• Never force your baby to go to a stranger or anyone else he seems afraid of.

• If a family member or friend seems upset because the baby rejected her, explain that your baby is just fearful of people he doesn't know well.

I Promise I'll Come Back

My daughter goes crazy if I try and go out without her. She throws herself on the floor and cries like I'm leaving forever. She won't even stay with her daddy anymore. It's driving me crazy because every time I need to run to the store to get milk, I either have to take her or go through this big drama. Sometimes I try and sneak out of the house when she's watching Barney. Should I do that or is it messing with her head?

Susan, 17 years old

✋ STOP AND THINK

Take a minute and discuss Susan's problem. How would you answer her question? Is it okay to sneak out of the house or should you tell your baby you are leaving?

Does your ten-month-old grab your leg and scream her head off if you try to go to the store without her? Does your sixteen-month-old put a death grip on your coat when you drop her off at daycare? Welcome to separation anxiety, another very normal and healthy part of your baby's growth. Even though it's frustrating, it only lasts until he's about two.

Why is your baby or toddler freaking out so much about your leaving? Well, there are a couple of reasons. Because you've been taking good care of her and building trust, she counts on you to help her feel safe. You're like her walking, talking safety blanket. When you leave, she feels vulnerable. The second reason is that she doesn't understand time. To her, leaving for ten minutes feels like you're leaving forever. She can't wrap her brain around the fact that you will return. The problem is that her separation fears might make you feel like a prisoner in your own home. Even though her clinging to your leg is normal, it can be hard to take. Here are a few things that can help.

Dealing with Separation Anxiety

- Separation anxiety is normal and good. It means your baby is attached to you.
- Remember, your baby isn't faking his fear just to get you to stay. He's really scared that you might not return. Talk to him. Reassure him you'll be back. Even if you don't think he understands, part of him does.
- Do some practice runs. Try going into a room next to the one he's playing in and letting him crawl to where you are. These little reunions help him learn that you aren't going to abandon him.
- When you do have to leave for real, have something ready for the babysitter to distract him with, like a new toy or a video. This will help shift his attention off you leaving.
- Never run out on your baby without saying good-bye. Taking off teaches him that he always has to watch you so you don't disappear.
- When you go out, always leave your baby with someone you can really trust. If he picks up on the fact that you don't feel good about the caretaker, his stress will increase.
- Leave with a smile and a kiss. This lets him know that everything is okay.
- When you get back, be sure to scoop him up and kiss him. Let him know you missed him.
- Your baby needs practice feeling safe when you're gone. Taking him everywhere you go all the time means he doesn't get a chance to master these fears. As long as he's with someone safe, it's okay to leave your baby—even if it feels uncomfortable for both of you!
- And remember, respecting your baby's separation fears is

not spoiling him! It's showing him that the world is safe and that his parent really "gets" what's going on inside of him.

So What is Spoiling?

I never got the love and attention I wanted from my parents, so I promised my baby she would get all the things I missed out on. But somehow, things got messed up. I make the same mistake over and over again. I spoil them and let them get away with whatever they want because I don't want them to hate me like I hated my parents. So I'm always trying to give my kids the things I never had. I have a hard time saying no, so I let them do as they please. I see how wrong this is and that I've made everything harder for me and my husband because we're always giving in to them. I don't know how to fix it.

Lisa, 18 years old

We have found that many people are really confused about what it means to "spoil" your baby. In truth, you can't really ruin anyone. But you can make some ineffective or misguided choices that lead to difficult behavior in your child. So we want to take this chance to lay it out. Like we said before, love never spoiled anyone. It's okay to think your baby is the most amazing, special, incredible, perfect person in the world! It's great to love your children as much as you possibly can. It's all good. Some people think that spoiling is just giving too much love. But that's not it at all. Respecting your baby's fears is not spoiling. So what is spoiling?

Stuff ≠ Love

First of all, "spoiling" really has to do with older kids, like from two years old and up. Because like we said before, babies cannot be spoiled. Spoiling can get played out in a couple of ways. Sometimes spoiling is giving kids things because you think it will make them feel loved (or make them love you). Or like Lisa said, giving them things to make up for what you missed. A better word for this is *overindulging*. Sounds like a big word, but it just means giving kids more than they need. When it comes to your kids, don't confuse things with love. Babies and young kids don't know anything about fancy sneakers, cool strollers, or expensive toys. All they need is your unconditional love and guidance. Buying kids every toy they ask for or candy every time they see it is overindulging them. And it's a bad pattern to get into.

If you felt cheated or deprived because your childhood was really hard, you might want to give your child those things to make you feel better about what you missed. But doing this is a trap. If you missed out on having caring, loving parents, material things won't make those feelings go away for long. Next time you get caught up thinking, "Oh my baby needs these really hot Nikes," ask yourself who it's really about. Material things can make you feel better for a while. They are a quick fix. But they aren't love. And love is what your baby or child needs. Not Nikes.

"Spoiling" also means letting your older baby or child do whatever they want. Sometimes this happens because you don't want to be harsh or mean like your parent was. Or maybe you just don't know how to handle a situation. Sometimes you get tired of battling with your kid to get him to do something (go to bed, do his homework, brush his teeth, pick up his toys). So you let things slide. This is spoiling. But a better word for it is *undisciplined*. Children need love and discipline. One without the other is no good. Discipline can be tricky to figure out. We'll talk about it more in another chapter.

A Special Note on Trust and Attachment

Although most babies form strong bonds to their parents, some don't. If your baby doesn't seem connected to you by the time he or she is a year old, it's very important you talk to your child's pediatrician about it. If you're having trouble explaining what's going on, just take this book and let the doctor read this paragraph. Your child's pediatrician will hook you up with a professional who can help you and your baby increase the bond. Don't worry, it doesn't mean that you did something wrong or bad. Sometimes it just takes a little extra work. But because this bond is so important, don't let embarrassment or shame stop you from getting help.

Chapter 5

Coping with the Stress of Parenting in Healthy Ways

My kids are the most important thing in the world to me. But right now I am sooooo stressed out. It's either they're crying or whining or running all over the house and waking up the neighbors who come up and scream at me to control my kids. My patience is very low right now, mostly because my son has been acting out real bad in school. I am about to flip out. What am I doing wrong??? I've been a mother for a few years now. You'd think I'd be used to this by now, but the stress still gets to me. I admit that sometimes I don't handle things right. I freak out at them, but I know it doesn't work. Like right now, I'm writing in this journal and they're destroying their rooms! What works best for me when I'm this stressed is to hide in the bathroom for five minutes and breathe. Sometimes I even do my deep breaths with my head out the window so I can get some fresh air.

Alexis, 22 years old

Every Parent in the World Feels Stress

There is no job in the world more stressful than being a parent. But look on the bright side—if you can do this, you can do anything! And it's not just because you're young that you feel stressed out over being a parent. **All parents feel stress.** But like we said before, being young, having the pressure of school, a job, and everything else that you have to deal with, can make parenting even more intense.

There are things about parenting that are tough, but knowing that every parent goes through them can make us feel less alone.

All Kids Get Sick

Yvonne's baby was born premature. Because of that he was often sick. He got colds and ear infections easily, and she had to take him to the doctor a lot. One day in the doctor's office, she told the pediatrician that she felt guilty, like it was her fault her son got sick so much. She felt like if she had taken better care of herself when she was pregnant, the baby wouldn't have been born early, and he wouldn't be sick all the time now. The doctor listened patiently, but told Yvonne that all babies get sick. Some more than others, but every child has his share of colds, bruises, and ear infections.

That's just life. It's sad, but our children will get sick and sometimes feel pain. Of course, it is very important to protect our children in whatever way we can, but sometimes no matter how hard we try, they get hurt. It's hard to see, but it doesn't mean that it's all our fault or that we did something wrong.

All Kids Act Up

I remember one time when my two girls pissed me off bad! They were at the food court in the mall. They were throwing sauce at each other, crying, kicking, and acting like fools. Everyone was staring at me. Judging me. The security guard came and said if I can't control my kids, I was going to have to leave. They said that my children were disturbing the other customers. I was angry at them, but mostly I was ashamed because I felt like people were looking at me saying, "Oh she's a young mother and she can't control her kids. She shouldn't have had them so young." When we got to the car, I just sat there and cried.

Lacy, 21 years old

No matter how well-behaved your children are, at some point they will embarrass you. Maybe they'll do it at school, in church, or at the supermarket. But it will happen. All kids act up. And when it does happen, just know that the world won't end. We aren't saying that you shouldn't teach your kids manners. We aren't saying that it's not important for them to follow rules (it is). But all children at one point or another will act badly. That doesn't mean you're a bad parent! And it doesn't mean that your kids are bad kids. It means that your children are children.

The Hidden Danger of Embarrassment

For some people, being embarrassed is a big trigger. If your child has done something to embarrass you, it is very important that you keep your cool. Don't fly off the handle and do something that you'll seriously regret. It will make a bad situation even worse. Take a moment and calm down before you discipline your child. Never touch a baby or child in the heat of the moment. It's too easy to snap. If you are really stressed or angry, follow the tips listed under Stress 911.

What Stresses You?

Take a minute and write down the three parenting situations that cause you the most stress. It could be getting your baby to bed. Or maybe it's dropping your child off at daycare. Is it having your mom tell you that you're not "doing it right" when it comes to your child?

Stress Scene #1_____

_____

_____

Stress Scene #2 _____

_____

_____

_____

_____

_____

Stress 911

A fight with your boyfriend might stress you. Your sister borrowing money and not paying it back might stress you. Losing your keys to the house might stress you. But your toddler having a temper tantrum for twenty minutes, while the noodles boil over on the stove, the phone is ringing, and your mother is yelling at you to make the baby stop screaming because the neighbors are banging on the ceiling, might call for emergency tactics. If you feel yourself going over the edge, you need to switch to emergency mode and try these tips.

Next time you're stressed and need to find the peace within you, try the ABC's of keeping your cool...

Always pause—before you do anything.

Breathe—until your body is calmer and
your mind is clearer.

Consider the consequences of your actions.
Choose carefully.

If you are boiling over, **don't handle your child**. Chances are you'll be rougher than you want to be.

If you can, get away from your child for a moment. It's better to put your baby in his crib for five minutes and shut the door than to wind up hurting him! But don't leave the baby alone for more than ten minutes.

Call someone right away who can help calm you—a friend, a sister, your mom. Don't call someone who might set you off even more, like a boyfriend or girlfriend who doesn't get how stressful raising kids can sometimes be.

If you have a friend or parent who can give you a break, let them. Get out of the house for a minute or two and clear your head.

Breathe, breathe, breathe. Deep breathing naturally calms the body. Take as many breaths as you need to feel more relaxed.

Counting to ten with each deep breath also helps. It gives you time to think.

Give yourself credit for keeping your baby safe. Nice job!

Your Emergency Plan

What is your plan for the next time you are at your breaking point with your child? Include at least three things you can do.

1. _____

2. _____

3. _____

Handling Everyday Stress

What works for me after a really stressful day is I get the baby in bed early as I can. Then I get in the tub and sit there for like an hour until my feet and hands get all like raisins. Even if the phone rings, I just sit in the tub. By now, my little brother has learned not to mess with me and try to get into the bathroom when I'm taking my bath. I'm serious! Then I get in bed and go to sleep. I'm telling you, when I come out it's like I'm a new person.

Gina, 17 years old

Ever notice how stress sneaks up on you? Little things get piled up until it feels like you have a fifty-pound bag of potatoes on your head. Here is a list of things you can do to reduce stress every day.

Stress Busters

- Get enough sleep and eat good food. Junk food drains your energy!

- Put your child on a regular feeding/sleeping schedule.

- Trade babysitting with safe/trustworthy friends.

- Meditate.

- Don't bring people into your life who are stressful and unhealthy.

- Be organized! An organized life is less stressful.

• Don't put off things you have to do. Tackle your responsibilities. It will make you feel more in control.

• Let people help you. Don't be too proud to accept help.

Have Fun

One of the best ways to beat stress is to do things that make you feel good. And we aren't talking drugs, alcohol, or other high-risk behaviors. Those might work in the short run, but they will leave you even more stressed when the high is gone. Here's a list of things that people do to make themselves feel good. Go through it and circle the ones that would work for you. Try to do a few of them every day!

1. Soak in the tub
2. Watch a good movie
3. Hang out with friends
4. Buy something (that won't make me broke)
5. Look at pictures of people I love
6. Sing or dance
7. Listen to music
8. Write in my journal
9. Talk on the phone
10. Eat my favorite food
11. Exercise
12. Get something done (clean out my closet, organize the baby's clothes)

13. Go to church, synagogue, mosque, or other spiritual place

14. Sleep

15. Cook an awesome meal

16. Do my hair or nails or go get them done

17. Eat out with a friend

18. Have fun with my child

19. Read to myself or to my child

20. Think positive thoughts about my future

21. Play cards with friends

22. Tell someone that I love them (especially my child!)

23. Remind myself of why I am a good parent

24. Buy or make a gift for someone

25. Be in nature

26. Think about a happy time in my past

27. Trying something new

28. Remind myself of my good qualities

29. Plan things in my future

30. Do something kind and generous for someone

(Linehan, 1993)

Meditation

At first I thought it was weird. But then I tried it. Since I've been meditating, I've been a much, much happier person. It helps me to think before I act and that's really important when you have a kid. Before I started meditating, I had a mad short fuse. But now, I don't snap so easily. It's like I have time to think about things before I react. It makes me a better, more calm parent.

Lisa, 18 years old

One of the best, most effective ways to reduce the stress that parenting causes is through meditation. You might be wondering what is meditation? Isn't it something that monks do? The answer is simple. Meditation is a way to get calm, centered, and focused. Like Lisa said, it gives you a longer fuse. And it's for anyone who wants to make their life less crazy and more peaceful. But the most important thing to know about meditation is that it only works if you do it!

How to Meditate

Simple Directions

1. Sit down

2. Be quiet

3. Pay attention to your breathing. Feel your belly rising and falling with each breath.

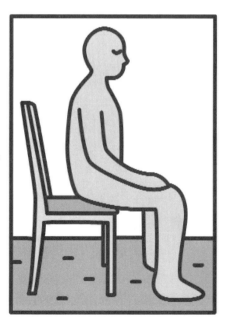

The Extended Play

1. Find a comfortable sitting position where your back is straight. Let your body be balanced and at ease. Place your hands comfortably on your lap or knees. Close your eyes. If you aren't comfortable closing your eyes, you can choose a place nearby and focus your vision in a relaxed way.

2. Bring your attention to your breathing. At first you can focus on your belly rising and falling. Notice the changing sensations in your body as you breathe in and out. Just feel your breath. Don't try to control it. Breathe naturally. Sometimes your breathing may be deep, sometimes it may be shallow. Your job is to simply be aware of your breathing and the changing sensations in your body as the air goes in and out.

3. Your mind will naturally wander away from your breathing again and again. When you realize your mind has drifted, just notice it with a "no big deal attitude" and return your attention to your breathing again.

4. After focusing on the belly for a while, you can expand your awareness to other parts of your body. Try feeling the breath as it comes in and out of your nose. Notice how the air is cooler as it comes in through your nostrils and warmer as it leaves. Again, remember, it's normal for your mind to sneak off into other thoughts. Just gently bring it back.

5. Do this every day. Shoot for at least fifteen or twenty minutes every day. If possible, choose a regular time. It makes it easier to remember.

Even if it feels weird at first, keep doing it.
Meditation works.

Meditating in the Heat of the Moment

Another way to use meditation is when you start to feel over-whelmed. Let's say that it's late in the afternoon and your child is tired, hungry, and really fussy. Maybe you're tired, too. Maybe she goes a step too far and does something that makes you really angry. Before you lose control, take a few minutes to pay attention to your breath. Breathe a few times, and as you breathe out notice the tension leaving your body. Where do you feel anger in your body? Just notice where the anger is hanging out. Now imagine breathing the anger out with each out breath. See it just evaporate into the air. With each breath find yourself stepping back from the edge of the cliff. Take a minute to let this calm feeling settle in. Every time you need to calm yourself down when parenting threatens to unglue you, try a mini-meditation.

Just Do it

Take a few minutes right now to focus on your breathing. Follow the direction written above. Once you've finished, write down how you are feeling. Relaxed? Calm? Anything else? Don't worry if it mostly feels strange at first. That will pass. Every time you need to find the peaceful, wise core of who you are, meditate!

*After my meditation I felt*_____

_____

_____

_____

_____

Thoughts and Stress

One of the most powerful discoveries that scientists have made about stress has to do with our thoughts. Did you know that the thoughts in your head can either make your stress level go up or go down? And what's even more important is that you control the thoughts in your head.

Let's say that there's a small fire in your backyard. It's getting close to the house. The first guy that comes along likes a lot of drama, so he pours gasoline on it. Instantly, the fire gets bigger, hotter, and more dangerous. Then another guy comes along (he likes being relaxed) and throws water on it. Soon the fire is gone. Well, we have the same power to make the stress in our lives big or small with the thoughts in our head.

Of course, our thoughts can't control all of our stress. But it can help more than you might think. Ever hear an adult say, "We were poor growing up, but we didn't know it because we never felt poor"? Well, it's true: how you look at your life determines how you feel about it.

The Dinner Test

Take 1: Imagine that your son spills his milk at dinner. Maybe it's the third time this week he's done it. Maybe you have thoughts in your head like this: This kid is totally out of control. He does this stuff on purpose. His cousin never acts like this. Why did I get this kid. I can't take it anymore. He's driving me crazy. If these are your thoughts, you will probably start to feel more stressed out.

Take 2: Now picture this. Your son spills his milk. This time you remind yourself how young he still is. You tell yourself that it's not the end of the world. Maybe he's not quite ready for a big kid cup yet. Oh well, no big deal. Like they say, "no use crying over spilled milk."

The point is...your thoughts have a big part in how you feel. Parents need to save themselves from drama. Why? Because babies and little kids don't like drama. They don't do well when things are tense, stressed out, or crazy. By keeping yourself calm, you can help keep your baby's world calm. Changing your thoughts is a big first step.

Take the Stress Less Challenge. Here are some examples of changing the thoughts in your head to reduce stress and tension. First read the stressful thought, then see if you can come up with your own Stress Less thought before you read the answer we give.

Stressful thought—This kid is always doing this.
Stress Less thought—Sometimes he doesn't listen to directions well. We need to work on that. But sometimes he does listen and I need to remember that, too.

Stressful thought—This kid is just like his father. He'll end up just like him.
Stress Less thought—I don't like it when he imitates his father's negative behavior. I have the power to teach him better behavior.

Stressful thought—I can't stand this whining for one more second
Stress Less thought – I wish he would stop, but it won't kill me if he doesn't. In an hour, whatever is happening now will be over!

Stressful thought—I have so much responsibility on me. It's too much.
Stress Less thought—Being a young parent can be tough, but I'm strong and I can do this!

Stressful thought—My mother did a crappy job raising me, so she has no right to tell me how to raise my kid.
Stress Less thought—I wish my mother wouldn't boss me around so much. But in the end, he's my child and I need to do what I think is right.

Give it a try. Pick one stressful thing that happens often while being a parent. Maybe it's the difficulty of putting your kids to bed. Or maybe it's having someone tell you that you're too young to be a good parent. First pick out a stressful thought that you might have told yourself in the past. Now think of a Stress Less thing you could say instead.

A situation that causes me stress is _____

_____

_____

_____

_____

_____

_____

The stressful thought that makes it worse is _____

_____

_____

_____

_____

_____

_____

The Stress Less thought I could say is _____

_____

_____

_____

_____

_____

_____

Chapter 6

Letting Go of Negative Feelings Toward Your Child

Last week I was going through a really hard time. It seemed like everything was going wrong. I was behind in school, I was late for work twice, and the daycare was angry because I picked her up late. Well, I walked into my mother's house because she was babysitting. And when my daughter saw me she just started screaming, "No, no! Get away from me. I don't want you. I want to stay with Grandma, not you." At first I just felt really sad. But she kept right on with it even after we left, and then I got pissed. Here I am busting my butt going to school and working and this is how she treats me? I was thinking how selfish she is and not grateful for what I'm trying to do. I was mad almost through dinnertime. Then I was like, "You know, she's only four. She doesn't know any better. She's just being how kids are. First they want this person and then that person." Seeing it that way made it easier to just let my anger go.

Alexis, 22 years old

Love My Kid? Are You Serious?

If someone asked us whether we loved our children, most of us would say, "Of course I do." We try to do right by them, make sacrifices, and express our love the best way we know how. But no matter how much we love them, all kids sometimes make their parents angry, frustrated, and upset. It's natural for this to happen. But as a parent, it's also important to learn how to let go of negative feelings and not let them build up and damage how you feel toward your child.

For children to develop and grow, they need to know that their parents are 100% on their side. That doesn't mean that you let it slide when he needs discipline or you cover his mistakes up (which means he won't learn from them.) What it does mean is that you see your child's Core Self. Remember we talked about the Core Self in chapter 3? It means that you see your child as an individual, filled with goodness and amazing potential. It means that you can see him make bad choices and see that he is not a bad child. For any child to do well in this world, he needs at least one person on his side. And that person is you. In this chapter we're going to look at some of the things that might keep us from being 100% on our child's side—and learn to let them go.

Dealing with a Difficult Baby

For the first three months, I couldn't get him to stop crying. I thought it was me at first, like I was bad at being a mother and wasn't taking care of him right. But then I just got fed up with it. Other people's babies would sleep and take a bottle like normal. Why wouldn't my baby? I even started feeling angry at him every time he cried, like "Uh-oh, not this again." The doctor told me the baby had something called colic and it wasn't my fault or his fault. That made me feel a little better, even though it was still hard. At least I didn't feel so angry anymore knowing that he wasn't just being bad.

Markesia, 15 years old

Did you know that some babies have a harder time getting comfortable? Some babies are startled by everything, are fussy eaters, and aren't easy to calm down when they are upset. Sometimes it's because they are born with colic (something that doctors don't really understand, but means that your baby might cry a lot and seem gassy. It usually ends at four months). Sometimes babies who are born premature or with other health problems might be harder to calm and soothe. Sometimes babies just take a while to get used to the world. But this doesn't mean that they are going to be "bad" children. A rough beginning isn't a vision of what's to come. And remember, she isn't doing this on purpose. She feels as bad or worse than you do, so don't hold a rough start against her!

Sometimes we can't change things about being a parent. Colic is colic and you just have to wait it out. But there are things we can do to make difficult times easier on ourselves and better for our children. If your baby has colic or trouble adjusting to the world, try these tips:

- Get her out of the house. Taking a fussy baby outside can sometimes stop a crying fit.

- Run the vacuum cleaner, a blender, a dryer, or any other machine in the house that makes "white noise." But not a loud stereo—this will not soothe her.

- If there's someone you trust who can give you a break—let them.

- If there's no one to help and the baby's been crying and you're at the end of your rope, put her in the crib until you get your balance back. Try breathing deeply to get calm.

- Remind yourself that no matter how bad the crying is, it won't last forever.

Don't Label Your Baby

It's really important when your child is going through a rough patch that you don't use this behavior to think of your child as "bad" or "difficult" or any other negative label that might stick around. From the very beginning, babies get a "rap." We've all heard people say things like, "Oh that's just Herman, he's one crabby child. Nothing pleases him." Or, "That's the little princess. She's gotta have everything her way." There are two big problems with labels. The first is that if a child hears the label enough, she will begin to believe it. And the more they hear these labels, the tougher they are to scrape off.

The second problem is that the people who use the label start to believe that it is absolutely true and treat the child that way all the time. The label blocks people for seeing the child in the moment for who she really is. **No child acts one way all the time.**

Billy was a two-year-old boy who had a lot of behavior problems. His mother, Erin, was called into the teacher's office at the preschool almost every day. She would be told that Billy hit other kids, took their food, and was really rough. Erin and Billy lived in a small apartment with a lot of people, including Erin's mother and Erin's three nieces and nephews. These were Billy's cousins and they were older and played really rough with Billy.

Every time Billy got in trouble at school, Erin's mother told her that Billy was "turning rotten just like his father." She said that Erin had a real "troublemaker" on her hands and she better get control of him soon. Erin knew that Billy's behavior was getting worse and she needed help. She talked to the teacher, who helped Erin and Billy get hooked up with a therapist. The therapist helped a lot. One of the best things that the therapist did was help Erin see what a wonderful, loving boy Billy really was. Erin had started to see Billy in one way: as a bully and a headache. But the therapist reminded her that he was a lot more than that. She also told Erin that it was important for her to catch Billy doing good things and praise him. As Erin started to see a different side to Billy, she saw beyond the bad labels. And she asked other people not to use these labels around Billy, too.

✋ STOP AND THINK

Think back to some of the labels that people might have put on you when you were growing up. How did these make you feel? Do you think these labels described the real you?

Don't Hold His Mom or Dad Against Him

I get so mad at my boyfriend for the things he does, like cheatin' on me, not giving me any money for the baby, and just other stupid stuff. I know it's wrong, but sometimes I hold it against my son for looking like his father or acting like him. I know he's just a baby, but I swear, sometimes they are just alike and that can be hard for me. Especially when I'm angry at my baby daddy. I shouldn't take it out on my son for all the bad things that his daddy does, but honestly, sometimes I do.

Charlene, 16 years old

Being a parent means that you're probably going to get angry about some of the things your kids do. **But sometimes we might find ourselves feeling angry at our children for things they didn't do and have no control over!** This can happen without us really even knowing that it's going on. And it's really, really important to pay attention to this, because it can end up damaging how your child feels about himself when he's older. Like Charlene said, if we are holding onto a lot of anger about our baby's other parent, we might find some of those bad feelings leaking onto the baby, especially if the child looks or acts like the other parent. It takes a lot of honesty to admit that our angry feelings for the other parent might affect how we feel about our child. But becoming aware of these feelings, if they exist, is the first step in letting go of them. When our child does something that reminds us of the other parent and we become angry or resentful, we can watch these feelings come up and then choose to let them go. We can say, "Hmm, remember that my child is his own person. He's not me or anyone else."

If we find ourselves saying to someone, "He acts just like his father!" or "He's going to end up just like his mother," we need to ask if this is helpful to our child. Is saying this being 100% on his side? Even if he does act like his father or mother at times, ask yourself what's the point of saying it? We find that it's more helpful to deal with the behavior that's causing the problem rather than blaming the parent for passing down the behavior through the bloodline! Here's how it might work…

Step 1—Let's say your child says, "I didn't do it!" when you catch him making a mistake. Instead of screaming, "You are lying just like your mother!" stop yourself (even if the thought comes into your mind).

Step 2—Remind yourself that your child is his own person. All children make mistakes. All children avoid the truth at one time or another. Keep your focus on your child, not the other parent.

Step 3—Deal with the behavior in the moment, without mentioning his parent who you aren't happy with. Calmly tell your child that you are going to give him a time-out or whatever discipline you choose.

Step 4—Congratulate yourself for keeping control of your feelings and handling the situation well.

By bringing our awareness to our angry and resentful feelings that have nothing to do with our child, we get control of them and get back to seeing who our child really is.

Little Kids, Big Ears

You might think that your baby is too young to understand what you're saying, but it's not true. Babies and children understand more than we think. Plus, you don't want other people (like cousins, aunts, or friends) to hear these labels and repeat them to your child. What your child hears from you about who he is makes a huge impression on how he sees himself. If he hears that he's smart, kind, funny, and fun to be around, chances are he'll believe it. If he hears that he's no good, a brat, selfish, greedy, or trouble, chances are he'll believe that, too.

Words have a lot of power. Use them carefully! This goes for things about your child's appearance, too. How many of us grew up feeling too fat, too skinny, too ugly, too "hyper," too short, or too tall because of things we heard people say about us? Of course, you can't always keep other people from saying things that might hurt your child. *But being 100% on your child's side means that your child doesn't hear these things from you!*

Take a moment and write down five positive qualities about your child. If your child is very young, write down some of the things (no matter how small) that you appreciate about him or her. Tell your child at least two of these things every single day. Keep the list growing as she does.

Five Amazing Things About My Child

1._____

2._____

3._____

4._____

5._____

Don't Hold it Against Your Baby

I'm kind of ashamed to admit it, but for a long time I was actually mad at my son for being born! Once he came, my life got harder. I felt so trapped. My boyfriend left me, my friends took off, and I had to deal with my mom being angry and dis-appointed that I got pregnant so young. Even though I loved my son, sometimes I would get angry at him and think, "If you weren't here, things would be a lot easier for me." I really love him with my whole heart. But there were times, especially at the beginning, when I really resented him.

Gina, 17 years old

Having a baby changes your whole life. And usually being a parent means that there's more stress and less opportunity to do what you want. At times we might even feel angry or resentful at our child for this. While those feelings are perfectly normal, it's important to be aware of them and to be very clear. **It's not your baby's fault that he or she is in the world.** It's just the way things are. If you feel angry or resentful thoughts toward your baby, check out the list below.

1. Congratulate yourself for noticing these feelings. Just being aware of these feelings is the first step in dealing with them in a healthy way.

2. Don't judge yourself for having these thoughts or feelings. It doesn't mean that you're a bad mother or a bad person. Feeling resentful from time to time doesn't mean you don't love your baby.

3. Talk to someone you can trust about these feelings. If these feelings become very strong or you feel very angry at your baby, get help right away. This means calling a safe, trusted adult who can help you get a plan together for keeping the relationship between you and your baby safe and healthy.

4. Remember that all feelings pass. Being a young parent can be very challenging. But both you and your child are growing stronger every day. We learn how to be effective parents—so soon the job will get easier.

Forgiving Your Child

One of the most powerful things you can do as a parent is to forgive your child. Actually, forgiveness is one of the most powerful things we can do for ourselves. When we forgive, we let go of the anger and resentment we are holding onto so we don't keep dragging it around. Forgiving our children is something we can do every day. It is a choice to see them for who they really are. By forgiving we see beyond their bad behavior, the mistakes they made, and the troubles they are experiencing (or causing). Forgiving means looking deeply to the core of who they are and saying, "I see the real you."

Forgiveness in Action

Here's an example of how forgiveness with your child might work. Let's say that your three-year-old has been going through a hard time. Maybe he's been acting out and getting in a lot of trouble. Imagine that he does something that is dangerous or aggressive, like hitting another child with a toy. This sort of thing has been going on a lot and you're getting fed up with it. It's important to understand that forgiveness is not pretending that our child's dangerous, inappropriate, or negative behavior is okay. Hitting requires giving him a time-out and telling him how wrong hitting is.

But forgiveness means that you also see the big picture. You see a frustrated three-year-old who can't quite figure out how to express himself effectively. You see a child who doesn't know a better way to get what he needs and ends up acting out and pushing people away, which probably makes him angrier. Sometimes these deeper, forgiving thoughts don't jump right out at us. It's easier to see a kid who's driving us crazy. That picture is right smack in front of us. But forgiveness asks us to see a different version of our child. A clearer and truer vision of who he really is. By practicing forgiveness, we see the true reality of our child—a wonderful little person who needs a lot of guidance and help.

 **STOP AND THINK**

Take a minute and, as honestly as you can, write down what you would like to forgive your child for. Maybe it's something about his behavior. Maybe it's because he was born with problems that require a lot of extra time and energy. Maybe it's because he keeps you from doing the things you'd like to be doing. Whatever it is, take a moment and forgive your child for these things. Take this time to see beyond whatever it is that needs your forgiveness and to appreciate the deeper part of your child.

I forgive my child for_____

I also forgive my child for_____

By forgiving my child, I let go of my feelings of_____

_____

Chapter 7

The Relationship with Your Baby's Dad or Mom

When I met my boyfriend, he seemed like another person than he does now. He always talked about finishing school and getting a good job. I told my friends he was so dependable. I guess he seemed different when he wasn't around his friends, and maybe I only saw what I wanted to see. We definitely didn't know each other enough. Now all we do is mess with each other. I talk trash about his mother and friends, and he tells me that I'm a shitty mother. It's bad. The problem is now we have a daughter. And one way or another, we're in each other's lives for the long run. One thing we do agree on, our daughter is not going to be raised without her dad involved in her life. So we're trying to work on our relationship. I don't know if we'll stay together or not. But we're in it for the long run as parents.

Denise, 20 years old

The One Thing You Can Be Sure of is That Nothing Stays the Same

If you are reading this book, chances are you met someone you were attracted to (at least temporarily), had sex, and ended up with a baby. You might still have a relationship with that person or you might not. Things change. Even if you fall madly in love with a person and stay together for a lifetime, things change. Typically, love starts with a wild attraction when you want to be together every minute. That attraction can be like a high or a rush, but eventually it fades. If the relationship is going to last and be healthy for the long run, it has to shift out of the fast lane and find a cruising speed. We call a relationship built on mutual respect, love, and empathy **nurturing** or **mature love.** This kind of love takes a lot of work. Mature love gives people a chance to grow and figure out who they are. Mature love is based on forgiveness and compassion. It is about friendship and dedication. You may be working toward this with your partner. Or you may not even be with your baby's other parent any longer.

In love and life things change. But one thing that never changes is that the choices you make like who you date, whether to live with someone, getting married, or staying out of relationships altogether impact your child. This chapter is designed to help you make healthy choices for you and your baby.

Just a note: People reading this book are probably in all different relationships. You might be married, seriously dating, or just hanging out. Rather than use the words husband, wife, girlfriend, boyfriend, or anything else, we've settled on "partner" to describe the person you're with.

Healthy Relationships

Have you ever been in an unhealthy romantic relationship? Anyone who has knows how hard it can make life. Being lied to, cheated on, disrespected, controlled, or hurt takes time and energy. Sometimes we get used to living on the roller-coaster of unhealthy relationships, but deep in our gut we know they're not good for us. In fact, unhealthy relationships can be very dangerous—for you and your child. Now that the safety and welfare of your baby is involved, it's your job to choose wisely. But some of us might never have seen a healthy relationship. Or we might have some fantasy idea from movies or TV about what a good, solid, decent relationship is. We asked some girls and guys about their ideas of what healthy relationships are made of. Here's what they said.

How People Act in Healthy Relationships

If you are in a relationship now, use this as a checklist and mark off any of the items that apply to your relationship!

- ❏ Not too controlling, like always wanting to know where you are and who you're with

- ❏ Shows you respect

- ❏ Listens to you when you have something to say

- ❏ Knows that you have a life that's not just him/her

- ❏ Supports you when you need it

- ❏ Not always nagging you about how you don't measure up.

- ❏ Accepts you for who you are

- ❏ Can say he/she is sorry when they mess up

- ❏ Generous with time and money

- ❏ Lets go of the little things and doesn't hold grudges against you

- ❏ Never uses violence on you

- ❏ Doesn't act all jealous when you talk to other people

- ❏ Lets you grow and change as a person

- ❏ Isn't always looking for some drama

- ❏ Doesn't always put what they want in front of what you want. Can compromise

 **STOP AND THINK**

Write down the top five things that you think are most important in a relationship. After you look at your list, ask yourself if the things you put on your list contribute to a healthy relationship. (For example, cute butt might be important to you, but is it part of a healthy relationship? Not necessarily!)

1._____

2._____

3._____

4._____

5._____

Are You in an Abusive Relationship?

Take the quiz below to find out.

1. I am afraid of my partner's temper. **Yes or No**

2. My partner yells at me, threatens me, or intimidates me.
Yes or No

3. My partner has kicked, hit, pushed, or thrown things at me.
Yes or No

4. My partner's jealousy is so bad that I'm afraid to hang out with other people. **Yes or No**

5. My partner has accused me of talking to or having sex with other people when I haven't. **Yes or No**

6. My partner tries to keep me away from friends and family.
Yes or No

7. I have been forced to have sex. **Yes or No**

8. I have to sneak around because I'm afraid my partner will freak out about where I've been. **Yes or No**

9. I worry about what my partner might do to me or my child.
Yes or No

10. After a bad fight with my partner he/she apologizes, says he/she loves me, and that it will never happen again. **Yes or No**

(Levy, 1993)

What's Your Score?

If you answered "yes" to questions three or seven, you are probably in an abusive relationship.

If you answered "yes" to any other questions, you may be in a controlling or abusive relationship.

The more questions you answered "yes" to, the more likely your relationship is dangerous to you and your baby.

If you are in a dangerous relationship, get help. If you have been too scared or confused to get out for yourself, do it for your child. If you are having a hard time leaving, ask yourself what harm might happen to you or your child before your partner changes. What will your child hear? What will your child see? What will your child feel? If you grew up in an abusive family, ask yourself honestly if this is what you want for your child.

AND REMEMBER!!! ABUSERS DON'T CHANGE UNLESS THEY WORK HARD. This might mean getting therapy, joining a group with other abusers, or getting help from a wise adult. Just going to jail will not change a person. Making promises won't change a person. Unless the abuser understands what he or she's doing is wrong, learns better ways to handle his or her anger and fear, and works hard to stop the abuse, **CHANCES ARE THE ABUSE WILL CONTINUE.**

Get a Safety Plan

If you and your child are in an abusive relationship and you haven't decided to leave, you **MUST** have a safety plan for when things get violent.

If violence breaks out, do your best to chill down the situation.

Do everything you can to get yourself and the baby out of the house safely.

Before the fight, identify a safe place where you can go (mom's, a friend's, or a shelter) where the abuser can't get to you.

(If you can) keep an emergency bag at your safe place. Or have a bag ready to go.

Call the police as soon as you are able to.

Children who grow up witnessing domestic violence are more likely to be abused or become abusers. It's that simple.

If you need help, go to a trusted adult or call a hotline number listed below. People will help you. Let them.

National Teen Dating Abuse Hotline: 1-866-331-9474

National Domestic Violence Hotline: 1-800-799-7233

Safe Horizon: 1-800-621-4673

National Runaway Hotline: 1-800-786-2929

(1-800-RUN-AWAY)

Not Cool in Front of Your Kid

My boyfriend and I are real careful about what goes on in front of my daughter. But one time I left her with my friend, and she and her boyfriend were having sex in the living room while my daughter was playing in the room next door. My daughter walked in the room and was just staring at them. Watching them have sex. My girlfriend told me this like it was no big deal. I was so mad. I am really strict about what my daughter sees and hears and then this happens! I think it upset my daughter a lot, too, because from then on she was doing all kinds of sexual acts between her dolls. I never let that friend watch her again.

Stephanie, 16 years old

What might not be a big deal to you can be scary, confusing, or upsetting to a baby or young child. As parents, it's our job to decide what our children will see and hear. **We can't control everything, but we can control a lot.** What are some of the things that you don't want your baby or young child to see?

- ✖ People having sex

- ✖ People fighting (shouting or using physical violence)

- ✖ A weapon like a knife or a gun

- ✖ Violence on TV

- ✖ Sexual behavior on TV or in magazines

✖ People using drugs or abusing alcohol in your house

✖ People talking about hurting other people

✖ Gang-related activities

✖ Other things_____

Fighting in Front of Kids

When my parents were married, they fought all the time in front of me and my sister. Maybe they did-n't realize how it made us feel. Maybe they didn't really care. But every time they started up, I got this sick feeling in my stomach like "here we go again." The strange thing is that I noticed me and my baby's father were doing the exact same thing! He'd come home late from work and I knew he'd been hangin' with his friends instead of home helping me. I'd get mad and just light into him big-time. Soon we'd be yelling and slamming doors. I guess I thought my daughter was too young to understand. But one *time me and her father were having a screaming match and I looked over and saw this scared look on her face. Then I knew that she was going through the same thing I did when I was little. That really made me think about what we were doing to her.*

Angela, 17 years old

In any relationship there will be times when disagreements or arguments happen. But what might seem like blowing off a little steam to you might feel scary and confusing to a child. The best approach is to not fight in front of your child. It's okay for children to see parents disagree if both people can express their differences in safe and nonthreatening ways. In fact, watching people disagree and resolve their problems peacefully teaches kids how to handle conflict.

But ask yourself, **"Is the way I'm acting now, the way I want to teach my child to handle conflict?" (Because that's exactly what you are doing!)**

If you know something may trigger an argument with your boyfriend or girlfriend, don't bring it up until you can talk about it in private. This can be hard to do because sometimes conflicts come up quickly. But having this plan in place will make things safer for your child.

Got Boundaries?

One time my boyfriend really wanted to go to the movies, but we didn't have a babysitter. Then a friend of his said that he and his girlfriend would watch the baby. I had a bad feeling about it because this friend wasn't so trustworthy. I knew he was messed up with some street stuff and I had a weird feeling in my gut. But my boyfriend laid this trip on me about how everything was always about the baby and I never made time for him. He threatened that if I wouldn't make time for him he would have to find someone else who would. We went to the movies, but I didn't have fun because I was worried the whole time. When we got back to the house, the girlfriend was gone because they had a fight and the baby was in the corner crying while my husband's friend and his boys were drinking beer and getting high. The baby probably sat there crying the whole time we were gone. I felt angry at myself and ashamed, like I put someone else ahead of my baby. But I learned from that. Never again.

Shana, 16 years old

As an effective parent, your number-one job is to keep your child safe—emotionally and physically. You and your child are a package deal now. Even if it feels uncomfortable, you have to draw boundaries with partners in order to keep your child safe. Sometimes it might feel like you're being pulled in a thousand different directions. But when it comes to safety, the needs of your baby should always outweigh the wants or needs of a partner. Take a deep breath. Think it through. Trust your gut. You and your baby will both be glad you did.

Not Together Anymore

If me and my baby's daddy broke up because he cheated on me, I would never let him see the baby. He made his choice, now deal with it! But if we broke up because things just weren't working out, then I guess I'd let him see our son. But I know I'll never have to worry about this because me and my boyfriend love each other and will be together forever.

Allysa, 15 years old

✋ STOP AND THINK

Take a minute and reread the quote from Allysa. Think about what she says. What do you think of her logic? Let's say that she and the baby's father do break up. What are the consequences for the baby if she never lets the father near their son? Is this fair to the child? Is this fair to the father? What is Allysa losing out on by making this choice?

One of the biggest questions we get during our parenting groups is about how to be a parent with an "ex." What's right for the baby? What if you and your ex don't get along at all? We strongly believe that it is possible to raise a baby with the other parent even if you're not together anymore. But it requires both of you to act as mature and level-headed as you possibly can. Some might say you have to step up to the plate, bite the bullet, turn the other cheek, be a bigger person, or just get the job done. It's not always easy to coparent with someone who has cheated on you, let you down, or made you angry. But having a working relationship will actually help you in the long run. And it will certainly help your child. Here are some tips to help you make the best of what can be a tough situation.

Not Knowing a Parent

So, why bother to work it out with an ex at all? Why not just give up all the headaches and move on? Well, if you grew up without one of your parents in your life, you know how much pain that can cause. You can't control it if your partner refuses to see the child, or goes to jail and is unavailable, or moves to another town. But you can work to make it possible for your partner to be involved in a healthy way in your baby's life. That might mean being the "bigger person" for the sake of the baby. If your baby's other parent is a safe and responsible person (and by this we mean will keep the baby safe while they're together), it's best for him or her to be in your baby's life. Period. Sometimes we tell ourselves, "Well, he (or she) doesn't give us enough money, he hangs out with his boys too much, he doesn't call us for weeks at a time, he makes promises he doesn't keep." All of this may be true. But is it important enough for you to keep your partner from being a part of the baby's life? NO!

Just because you might be angry at him doesn't mean your child should have to be. Don't ruin her relationship with her other parent out of your own hurt and anger. That means no nasty faces when his name comes up, no hanging up the phone when he calls, and no badmouthing him. Research shows that kids who constantly hear their dad or mom is bad, think they are, too, because their parent is part of them. You're not doing it for him. You're doing it for your kid.

Knowing Her Dad Will Make Her a Healthier Kid...

Did you know that kids who know their dads

- ✔ do better than average on tests that show how they are growing and learning
- ✔ are less likely to run away
- ✔ are much less likely to be violent, dangerous, and even criminal
- ✔ are better at doing things without help, keep control of themselves, wait longer before they start having sex
- ✔ are more likely to go to school, stay in school, and not repeat a grade

Boys who grow up without a father are 300% more likely to be put in a state juvenile institution.

(Healthy Families San Angelo, 1992)

 **STOP AND THINK**

If you grew up with only one parent or two parents who were always fighting, how did that make you feel? Or maybe one of your parents was always trashing your other parent. What kind of position did that put you in? How can you prevent your child from going through the same things?

Being a Parent isn't 50/50

It just doesn't seem fair. We both made this baby, but I'm the one who does all the work. I have to stay home at night while he goes out with his friends. Plus, we both have jobs, so why does all my money go to the baby and his money goes to whatever he wants to do?

Gina, 17 years old

We go through life being taught to make things fair. But when it comes to being a parent, things aren't always fair. If you are expecting the other parent to do as much as you (the primary care-taker), you will feel angry and disappointed a lot of the time. Guaranteed. If you get stuck in the anger for too long, you begin to pass up moments of happiness and joy. Soon, you may find yourself reacting to these negative feelings, rather than acting on what is best for your child!

Don't let "fairness" be a reason for keeping the other parent out of your baby's life. If you use the baby as a bargaining chip, everyone will lose. For example, if you keep the other parent away from the baby because he or she isn't pulling his or her weight, you are training the other parent to stay away. If you make conditions about seeing the baby that he can't realistically meet, you are pushing him away. Sure it would be nice if they paid their share, did as much childcare, and washed as much laundry as you. But sometimes to be more peaceful and make healthy choices, we have to ignore the score.

Here are some reasons NOT to limit your child's access to a parent.

Doesn't give as much money as you think is fair

Doesn't parent the way you do (but is safe)

Doesn't visit or take the baby as much as you want

Has a girlfriend/boyfriend you don't like

Has more free time than you do

Let's be clear. You have the right to ask the baby's other parent for what you want and what you think is fair. You have the right to tell the other parent what's on your mind. But the main question you should ask when making choices about your ex is "What's best for my child?" Pushing the other parent out of your baby's life leaves you with more work, more anger, and a child who sees less and less of his other parent.

Talking in a Way That People Will Listen

I get so freakin' angry at my baby's father. And trust me, there have been plenty of times when I have just screamed at him until my head almost exploded, like when he said he would pick the baby up and then never showed. One time I waited for him so I could go to work and he was almost two hours late. But the more I screamed and yelled, the more he tuned me out and the less he took the baby. It got to the point where I was so angry at him, there was nothing he could do right. So I tried something I learned from my mother's group. It's called the Oreo. First I give him the cookie-sort of like a compliment. "Gary, you know you can be a really good dad a lot of the time. When you're with Brianna you take good care of her." This opens up his ears 'cuz he's hearing something he does right. Then I give him the cream-something I want him to change. So like, "But I really need you to get here on time so I'm not late for work. We need this money." Then I give him the second cookie. "I'm glad you try hard to be a good dad. Not a lot of other guys do as much as you." Sometimes it's hard to come up with the cookies, especially when he's being a jerk and I want to rip his head off. But I know he listens better and doesn't tune me out when I do. And me getting' what I want is a good thing.

Shaniqwa, 19 years old

The Oreo

One of the best ways to make things work out the way you want is to be an effective communicator. That means talking in a way so people can listen. You might be justified in being angry or pissed off. But how you express that to the person you are upset with determines whether you'll get what you want. If you start screaming at someone, telling him what a no-good, loser parent he is, chances are he'll either tune you out, scream back, or not show up very much. Now you're feeling even angrier, right? But what if you figured out a way to get him to really listen and understand what you or the baby needs and why it's important? Think of an Oreo cookie: chocolate cookie—cream center—chocolate cookie. Believe it or not, an Oreo cookie can help us be a more effective parent!

Example: Let's say your baby's dad was supposed to watch the baby for you while you went out with a friend. You'd been planning this for a week and you were really excited about it. When he finally does show up, he's an hour late and your friend went to the movies without you. You're really steamed. Instead of blowing up and getting into a fight that leads nowhere, try giving him an Oreo.

Before you try this, make sure you are calm and in control of your feelings. Here's how it works:

Cookie #1—Give a compliment—even if you're angry at the person. Sounds crazy, but it works. The best way to capture anyone's attention is to start off by saying something that's nice (and also true) about them. If you start with a criticism, he or she will get defensive and the conversation will turn into a battle. Start with something he does do right. Example, "You know, Darryl, you are really good with Orlando. And when you're with him, I know he's safe and happy."

The Cream Filling—Tell the person how you feel and what you want to have happen. Use "I" statements. Don't start blaming or shaming. Stick to the facts. It helps keep the conversation on track. For example, "I'm so disappointed and frustrated. It's really important for me to have some time to go out, too. I take care of the baby a lot and sometimes I need a break. When you promise to take care of Orlando it's really, really important that you show up on time." Stay away from statements like "you always" or "you never."

Cookie # 2—End it with another compliment or something that is good about the person and true. Example, "I'm glad you want to help out with Orlando. He's lucky to have both parents in his life."

WARNING!!! Oreos take practice. It might feel weird to do this at first. You might be saying, "Is she crazy? Give a compliment when he screwed up?!?" But this is an effective way to get what you want in the future. It also gets you in the right mental space to speak and act calmly. **You can't get to a good place in a bad**

way. And Oreos work with all people, not just your baby's other parent. Use it with your own mom, dad, sister, or whoever else you need to live with. It doesn't solve all problems, but it does make life a whole lot less dramatic, which is good for you and your baby.

Tips on How to Deal with Conflict

- Stay calm.

- Use the Oreo technique.

- Stick to the point. What do you want to have happen?

- Don't attack the other person. Use "I" statements. Talk about how you feel, not what a jerk the other guy is.

- Don't threaten to keep the person away from the baby (unless he is acting unsafely). He might take you up on it!

- Be realistic. Don't always ask for more than the other person can give.

- Live in the moment. Don't get stuck in old battles.

- Allow him or her to change. If the other parent starts to be a more available or reliable parent, give credit where credit is due!

- Remind yourself: you have the power to choose from moment to moment how you want to deal with anger and conflict. Pat yourself on the back every time you make a choice to walk away from unhealthy patterns.

Take a moment and fill in the Oreo chart below.

OREOs

Think back to a conflict that you have had with your baby's other parent. Describe what happened and how you felt._____

_____

_____

_____

_____

Cookie #1. Write down a true and believable thing about the other person that has something to do with the problem you are having. For example, if your baby's father forgot to bring the diapers he promised, don't tell him he's a great artist. Tell him, "I know you care a lot about your daughter."_____

_____

_____

_____

_____

_____

The Cream Filling. Using "I" statements, tell how you feel, what you want to have happen, and why this is a good thing for your child. _____

_____

_____

_____

_____

_____

_____

Cookie # 2. Say another cookie, just to keep him or her listening and on track. It can be the same as cookie #1.

_____

_____

_____

_____

Practice this with a friend or trusted person so that it's ready to go next time a conflict pops up!

The next section of this chapter includes some letters from moms and dads to each other. We tried to pick letters that didn't just bust on the baby's mom or dad, but expressed the experiences, hopes, plans, fears, thoughts, and feelings that many young parents have. Do they bring up some of the issues or feelings that you have?

Letters from Moms to Dads

Dear Juan,

When I think about us and our baby I am so happy 'cause even when things are hard we still have such a beautiful baby and she is the reason I live and the air I breathe and I know that you feel the same way. I can't imagine life without you or her. You know, I really wish that we didn't fight so much and that you could be a little more mature. I hope that in time we will grow to be a very happy family. I know that sometimes I'm a little dramatic and sometimes I act crazy at you, but I feel like we need to work this out for Gina. Our daughter needs you and she loves you. She needs you to be a man and so do I.

Alexis, 22 years old

Dear William,

I'm writing you this letter to tell you how I feel about being a mom. From the day we found out that I was pregnant, I never thought we would be going through what we are going through right now. From the day we decided to keep our baby we had so many plans, and I'm not trying to sound mean but part of our plans wasn't for you to be in jail and me being out here doing everything by myself. I know when you was out you was doing the right thing—you got a job, took care of the baby.

You played with him. You're an awesome father but you made a lot of mistakes. It bothers me a lot but most of all it hurts me because of the baby. Because of the mistakes you made my son can't be with his father and it hurts. When I take him up there and when we walk out he always looks back at you like he's waiting for you to get up and walk out with us, and he keeps on looking until he can't see you no more and that just wants to make me break down and cry.

And now I'm out here doing every thing by myself. I have to work about a ten-hour day most every day to support our son. I have to pay all the bills by myself. I have to take care of Carlos by myself. I have to deal with daycare when Carlos acts up. I have to do everything by myself and it hurts me and stresses me out to the point that sometimes I feel like I can't handle it. I didn't make him by myself so why should I have to raise him by myself? I don't want to hurt your feelings but it's true. I know when you come home you're going to do the right thing but if you ever think about messing up again, think about the baby and how he is losing out on not having his father around. Because boys need a father figure more than they need a mother figure. My life has changed so much in so many ways. I really never thought my life would be like this. But it's something that I need to suck up and deal with. I'm not able to go out and just have time for myself. Sometimes I even have a hard time finding a babysitter to watch him while I'm working.

Don't get me wrong, I love my son with all my heart. He's the best thing that has ever happened to me and I thank you for that. I'm happy that I had my son with you. I wouldn't want to have a baby with no one else. You're a great dad, and when you want to be you're a good boyfriend. You stood by me through my whole pregnancy. But I wish you just would have listened so you could be here today. I always knew what was going to happen when I became a mom. It's a lot of responsibility but I wouldn't change it for anything. My life has changed in so many ways but even though I'm struggling right now I wouldn't change it besides having you home.

Erin, 19 years old

Dear Michael,

I'm writing you this to let you know how I feel. First, let me say that I really do appreciate how you are there for us emotionally. In the beginning I had to do everything for the baby like feeding him, changing him, bathing him, and being with him all day. You changed all that when you moved in with me and my mom. I am thankful about how much you help take care of our son.

But I'm scared and stressed out because you don't keep a job for more than a few weeks. I feel like all the financial problems is on me and it scares me. I never get to spend any of the money on myself because the baby takes it all. I don't get to fix myself up like I used to. And so I go around feeling like a bum. Plus I wonder where you get the money you spend on clothes and eating out? On second thought, maybe I don't want to know. But tell me this, What do you want to do with your life? What happened to your dreams of getting your GED and going to college? You can't just hang out with your friends on the corner and watch life pass you by. I'm worried about our future and I want to make sure that we have one. A good one. I hope you read this and we can sit down for a serious talk about where we're going.

Angela, 17 years old

Letters from Dads to Moms

Dear Patricia,
Becoming a father at such a young age was very hard for me especially since I never had a father figure or any role model for what a father was supposed to act like. I came from a very abusive house and I didn't always know right from wrong or how to deal with my feelings. I still remember going online to try and learn about taking care of the baby and getting her shots and how to put her to sleep. There's a lot I still don't know. But what I do know is that I want something different for our daughter. I know we aren't together anymore, but that doesn't mean I shouldn't be allowed to be there for our daughter. She's the only thing I have right now, and I feel like you

do things to make it harder for me to be her father. Since you got a new boyfriend it's like I don't exist. And the only time you call me is when you want something. But when I need something from you, it's like you don't listen or care.

I know we went through some bad times together. And I'm sorry for what I did, hurting you like that. It wasn't all good times, that's for sure. But now I feel like you're taking it out on me by keeping me from my daughter. Because that gives you control over me. And it's wrong to use our daughter like that. It hurts me, but it hurts her too. I don't want her to suffer like I did when I was young. I want us to work together to give her the kind of life we never had. We can't keep hurting her. Thank you for reading this letter. Please kiss our daughter for me.

Jon, 22 years old

Dear Giselle,

I can't tell you how scared I am to be having a baby. I still feel so young. I haven't finished school, I got no job, we're still living with my mother, and I don't know how we're ever gonna afford a place of our own. And I got to be honest with you. I feel like you pushed me into having this baby and I don't really like that feeling. I told you I wasn't ready to be a dad, but you went right ahead with keeping the pregnancy. I feel like I had no real choice in this matter and then you act pissed off that I'm not more happy about it. Well the truth is, like I been telling you that I wasn't ready for no baby and now in six weeks I'll be having one regardless. I love you and I love the baby already. I will do everything to support you both. But I just want you to know how I feel about this in my heart.

Trevon, 16 years old

Dear Stephanie,

I am writing this letter to tell you that I think you are a good mother to our son. You take really good care of him and I know he's growing up right. But I need to get some things off my chest. Sometimes I feel like I can never do anything right in your eyes. You're always telling me that I don't give enough money to you and that you and the baby have to go without. But I am doing the best I can and holding nothing back. But you act like I'm cheating you. Sometimes I feel like all you want me for is the money. And that really hurts me because I try to be there for you and the baby emotionally.

Also, I feel like nothing I do with the baby is right. Even when I change her diaper, you say it's not on and now it's gonna leak. Or that I don't burp her the way she's used to. Or that the clothes I choose aren't the right ones. Or whatever. You just make it so hard sometimes that I don't want to be here. But then again, I don't want to miss out on time with our daughter.

Sometimes I just wish you would say that I did something right or give a nod to what I'm trying to do. Why does everything have to be a battle with us?

Thank you for reading this letter. It means a lot to me. And I just want you to know how much I care for you and the baby.

Juan, 18 years old

Write Your Own Letter: Take a moment and write a letter to your baby's mom or dad. What would you like him or her to know about what it's like for you to be a parent. How has your life changed? What hopes do you have for your baby? What are your ideas about how to make those wishes into a reality?

Moving On

Personally, when I first start talking to someone, I never let them near my child. I don't want to confuse my baby with guys coming in and out. Not that I'm with so many guys. But you know what I mean. I like to keep it clear. Nobody is meeting my child the first time we hang out.

Latisha, 17 years old

At some point, if you don't stay with your baby's mom or dad, you'll probably start seeing other people. Dating once you have a child is a whole different ballgame than dating when it's just you.

And to keep things safe and smooth, it helps to create some guidelines about what's acceptable and what's not. Here are some thoughts from other young parents about dating. After each letter, take a look at the questions and think about them.

One thing I don't like is if a guy tries to discipline my child when I haven't even been with him for that long. You're not my baby's daddy, so don't act like it. I'll do the discipline unless we get serious and then we can have a talk about it if things are gonna change in that department. But until then, disciplining my child is my job.

Angela, 16 years old

What's Angela's concern with a new boyfriend?
How does she decide to handle it?
Do you agree or disagree with Angela's choice? Explain.

I started talking to this new girl and pretty soon we were seeing each other a lot. I'm not with my baby's mama, but we see each other almost every day because I take my daughter while her mother goes to work. Well this new girl, she didn't want me to see my daughter because she was jealous of the baby's mother. She was always trying to mess up me going to get my daughter, so one day I just told her flat out that she needed to stop that. I'm not with the mama, never going to be with the mama, but I am going to see my daughter.

James, 19 years old

What's James's concern with his new girlfriend?

How does he decide to handle it?

Do you agree or disagree with James's choice? Explain.

I started dating this one guy and he seemed pretty nice. He was always so polite to my mother and thoughtful, like bringing flowers or some other little thing. But the more we hung out, the more I saw this other side to him. He became more physically aggressive with me and controlling. Also it became clear that he wasn't in it for the whole package. He wanted me, but not my son. One time we got into a fight and he grabbed my arm and twisted it. My son who was three at the time ran over to try and protect me. Well, this guy grabbed my son and threw him across the room. Let me tell you, that was the last time that S.O.B. ever came into my house.

Diamond, 18 years old

What's Diamond's problem with her boyfriend?

What other problems are there?

How does she decide to handle it?

Do you agree or disagree with Diamond's choice? Explain.

The guy I'm with now is great. I think my baby's father knew that the relationship was serious. And that made him mad jealous. One day he told me that he forbid me to bring my son around my boyfriend.

I couldn't believe he was for real. But every time the baby's father was around he'd say, "You better not bring that guy near here or I won't give you another dime." It was crazy stuff. I tried to keep things cool, but I kept right on seeing my boyfriend. Things got easier when the baby's father found a serious girlfriend. He left me alone about it after that.

Janet, 18 years old

What's Janet's problem with her new boyfriend?
How does she decide to handle it?
Do you agree or disagree with Janet's choice? Explain.
What would you have done?

Take a minute and think about what's important to you when it comes to being with someone who's not your baby's parent. Look at the questions below and come up with your game plan.

The New Relationship Game Plan

What kind of person are you looking for? (Think back to some of the healthy relationship characteristics from the beginning of this chapter.)

When would you want your new boyfriend/girlfriend to meet your child (if he/she doesn't know your child already)? Right away? After a few weeks? A few months?

How much involvement do you want this person to have with your child?

How do you want them to act toward your child? Be specific.

What is not okay for your new boyfriend/girlfriend to do or say around your child?

How would you feel if your new boyfriend/girlfriend disciplined your child?

How will you deal if the baby's mother or father gets jealous?

Chapter 8

Just for Dads

Why Dads Matter (Big-time)

Here are a few facts you might not know about kids who grow up with a dad!

☛They are more likely to be active, healthy, and strong babies, toddlers, preschoolers, and school-aged children

☛Most of them do better than average on tests that show how they are growing and learning

☛Girls do better in math

☛They are less likely to run away

☛They are much less likely to be violent, dangerous, and even criminal

- Boys and girls are better at doing things without help, keeping control of themselves, and being better leaders. They are more successful in life
- Teens wait longer before they start having sex
- Children are more likely to go to school, stay in school, and not repeat a grade
- Girls have healthier relationships later in their lives, especially with men. Remember that Dad is the first man they get to know
- Boys who grow up without a father are 300% more likely to be put in a state juvenile institution

(Healthy Families San Angelo, 1992)

So You're a Dad Now

Congratulations! Becoming a father is an awesome experience. And you are probably feeling a lot of different things. Some dads are excited from the first minute they hear the news. Some guys tell us that they didn't really plan on it or that they were caught by surprise. Some need a little time to get used to the idea. A lot of guys notice their feelings change once they see their baby and get connected to him or her. All of these feelings are normal and okay. Being scared or upset at first doesn't mean you're not cut out to be a dad! Here is a list of how some young dads felt when they first found out they were having a baby.

Scared, Nervous, Excited, Confused, Happy about it, Trapped, Like I wasn't ready for the responsibility, Freaked out, Like I didn't want to have a baby, Real good, Under pressure to provide for the baby and my girl, Like it was a mistake, Good because it helped me straighten my life out, At first I was against it, but now I'm getting more pumped up as the baby gets closer to coming.

How did you feel when you first found out you were having a baby? Did these feelings change over time? _____

_____

_____

_____

_____

No Role Model

To be honest with you, I didn't know how to be a dad. My father split when I was a baby and my mom raised me alone. My mother's brothers were around a lot and they stepped in to help us out. But it's not the same as having your own dad around. I always felt like a piece of my life was missing on account of having no father figure. So from the second my girl told me she was pregnant, I knew there was no way my kid was going through the same thing. At first I wondered what exactly a good father is supposed to do. I started reading books and checking things out online. It helped me, but there's still a piece of me that thinks I would have been better off at being a dad if I had had one myself. That won't stop me from *trying my best though, 'cause my kid comes first. And I'm not ever walking out of her life.*

Brian, 20 years old

The best way to learn to be a dad is to look around you. Find a role model (a relative, neighbor, or family friend). Watch them, ask them questions, and do what they do. There are other ways to learn to be a dad, too. Read a parenting book (like this one!). Go online. Get hooked up with a parenting class. But more than anything else, just spend time with your child and treat him or her the way you would want a dad to treat you! Be a good listener, play with him, think about his feelings, protect him, respect his mother.

If you grew up without a dad in your life, you're not alone. Lots of people are raised by just their moms or by their grandmothers. And although this might make you unsure of how to be a dad, that doesn't mean you can't be a great one. Being a dad just means showing up emotionally, physically, and financially. You don't have to be perfect. You just have to be there!

✋ STOP AND THINK

If you grew up without a father in your life, take a moment and write down how this made you feel as a child. Now that you're a dad, what would you like to say to your father? What questions would you like to ask him? If you did have a father in your life as you grew up, ask yourself how your father influenced the kind of dad you are or want to be. What would you like to do the same as your dad? Or different?

_____

_____

_____

Being a Dad is incredible (But Not Always Easy)

We all want the best for our children. We want them to have more than we did as kids. Most of all we want them to be happy. When we first hold our babies, we look at them and have hopes and dreams for how their lives will be. Unfortunately, things don't always work out the way we plan. We might even find ourselves spending less and less time with our children as time goes on. This happens for a lot of reasons. And it's important to figure out what's making us check out from our kids so we can solve the problem and start showing up. Here are some things that young dads said made it hard to be the kind of dad they wanted.

- Not getting along with the baby's mother and staying away to avoid fights

- Wanting to be more involved, but feeling pushed away from the child by the baby's mother

- The baby's mother's new boyfriend doesn't want me around

- Feeling like the only thing I'm good for is giving money. And most of the time I don't have any. So what's the point of going over just to be yelled at?

- The baby's mother makes me feel like I don't know how to take care of my child

- Sometimes I'm not sure what to do with the baby like when she cries or gets sick

- My new girlfriend is jealous of the baby's mother and doesn't like it when I'm over there

- I got so much pressure trying to go to school and work. By the time I get home, the baby is asleep

 **STOP AND THINK**

For each of the problems in the list, think of a peaceful, reasonable solution. If you're having trouble getting along with the baby's mother, read the section on Cookies on pages 98-100. Sometimes dads need to go to court to make sure they get the visitation rights they deserve. If you're feeling unsure of how to care for your baby, ask someone or read a book. Nothing is worth stepping out of your child's life. Every problem has a solution.

Keep Your Eyes on the Prize

I'm not with my baby's mother anymore, but I will always be my son's father. Sometimes me and her get into it. And more than once she's tried to use my son against me, saying, "If you don't give me this or do that, I won't let you see your son this weekend." At first it used to drive me crazy and I was like, screw you, then I'm not comin' over there. But then I saw that it just hurt the baby. We were so caught up in our anger for each other that we were hurting our son. Now I try to take the high road. She pisses me off, but I keep focused on what's most important. Not her. Not me. My son.

Eric, 21 years old

No one can replace you. Your child only gets one dad and you're it. No matter what's going on in your life, your child will never really understand why you weren't there. Plus, a lot of times kids grow up blaming themselves for why a parent didn't show up. Nobody wants their child to feel like that. When things get hard, keep your eyes on the prize—your child. If you've already missed out on time with your child for whatever reason, don't let that stop you from connecting now. You may need some time to get used to each other, but soon spending time together will feel completely normal. You mean more to your child than anyone else in the world. You don't have to be rich, you don't have to drive a BMW, you don't need to be a doctor or a lawyer, you don't need to be tall or handsome. All you have to do to be a hero is show up day after day.

Note: If you're a dad and only read this one chapter, we invite you to read the rest of the book. It might seem like it was written mostly for moms, but that's because moms often (but not always) take care of the baby a lot of the time. But every chapter in this book is filled with information that can help you be the best parent possible whether you're a mom or a dad. So read on!

Chapter 9

Full House—Raising a Baby with Your Family

It's tough trying to raise your baby with your mom. It's hard to know who the real boss is. In a way, I thought that the baby would bring us closer together because we've never gotten along that great. But really I can see that it's just given us one more thing to fight over. At times, though, I look at her and the baby and I know that they love each other. She takes care of him a lot when I'm at school, so they're real tight. That's a load off my mind, because no matter how much we fight over the right way to do this or that, or who's the boss when it comes to the baby, I know I'm not in it alone.

Latisha, 17 years old

Are you raising your child with your mother, grandmother, or other family members? Does the baby's other side of the family help out? Many young people wouldn't be able to take care of their children without the support they receive from their families. At the same time, raising a baby with your family can bring up old issues, cause new conflicts, and require a lot of patience on all sides. This chapter talks about some of the trickiest parts of raising a baby with your family and what you can do to make it the most positive experience possible.

***In this chapter, we use the word "mother" to mean any family member who is helping you raise your child. It could be someone in the baby's other parent's family, an aunt, grandmother, cousin, or stepmother.

Support from Mothers and Others

Becoming a mother helped me and my mother get a lot closer. Before she was never there for me. I felt a lot of anger toward her about how she raised us. I wanted to be close to her, but my anger made me pull away. It was kind of like, "You were never there for me before, so you have no right telling me what to do or how to act. You lost your right to do that by checking out on me." But now the baby's here and my mom's really different. She helps me out and looks out for me and the baby, which is good since the baby's daddy is out of the picture. I think she's trying to make up for how she raised me. But I'm leaving all that in the past. Because really, I don't know what I'd do without her now.

Denise, 20 years old

Maybe you were already on good terms with your mother when you found out you were pregnant. Or maybe you hadn't been close, but you both put aside past arguments and disagreements when you found out that you were pregnant. We are definitely not suggesting that you get pregnant in order to work things out with your mom, but sometimes having a new child in the family can offer a new start—with your family and your partner's family. There can be a lot of benefits for you and your baby, too. Reconnecting with family means you have a larger support network. The baby will grow up knowing his family. (Cutting off from family is almost never healthy unless the people are physically or emotionally harmful. And keeping your baby connected to his or her relatives is a gift that only you can make happen). If at all possible, make a promise to use your baby's arrival as a chance to reconnect and heal old wounds.

A New Start

Carrie was never very close to her boyfriend's mother. Mrs. Santiago told her son, Juan, that Carrie was no good for him. It seemed to Carrie that her boyfriend's mother was just possessive and didn't think that any girl was good enough for her son. The whole time Carrie was dating Juan, Mrs. Santiago had an attitude toward Carrie and didn't want her around. In the back of her mind Carrie also thought that Mrs. Santiago didn't like her because she wasn't Hispanic.

When they broke the news to Mrs. Santiago that Carrie was pregnant, it was a disaster. Mrs. Santiago cried and screamed that Juan's life was over and that she always knew that Carrie would mess him up.

As Carrie's due date got closer, Mrs. Santiago's attitude started to change. She began to get excited about having her first grandchild. But still, Carrie didn't want anything to do with her because of how Mrs. Santiago had treated her in the beginning.

The baby was about six months old when Juan got sent to prison on an old charge he had before he met Carrie. Carrie was all alone and trying to raise the baby and go to work. At first she didn't want Juan's mother's help because she was still angry, and keeping Mrs. Santiago away from the baby was Carrie's way of getting back at her. But one time Carrie got really sick and had no choice but to let Juan's mother take care of the baby for a few days.

From that point on, things changed. Carrie let Juan's mother help out more and more. It let Mrs. Santiago feel closer to her son and grandson, and it gave Carrie the break she needed. It wasn't always easy to let Mrs. Santiago have a hand in raising her son, but Carrie knew that it was good for everyone. After that, Mrs. Santiago treated Carrie better and Carrie was able to get past a lot of her hard feelings.

Sometimes having a baby can be a positive fresh start for people like it was for Mrs. Santiago and Carrie. Putting aside small grudges, old conflicts, and hard feelings for the sake of the baby is usually a win-win choice. However, you should **never bring some-**

one into your child's life if they are unsafe to you or your child. If you haven't been in touch with a parent because he or she abused you, it's your job to keep your baby safe from this person, too. Until you are absolutely sure that this person will not be abusive again, neither you nor the baby should be around him or her.

Reaching Out Doesn't Always Go Both Ways

Unfortunately, just because you are mature enough to reach out to parents or other relatives doesn't mean that they will be mature enough to respond with love and support. If you try and reconnect with a parent and they react to you with hostility, shame, silence, or anger, just know you did the wise thing. Sometimes parents don't come around and this can really hurt. It can reopen past wounds and remind you of how your parents might not have been there for you in the past. These are normal feelings, so be patient with yourself. In your heart, be clear that you did the right thing. And in the back of your mind, keep open to the idea that the separation might be temporary.

Sometimes people have dreams or fantasies that having a baby will bring their family back together. Sometimes this happens, but a lot of time it doesn't. Or your parents might offer to help, but not the way you had hoped for. As you've probably figured out, you can't control how your parents treat you. You can't control how supportive or nurturing they are. You can't control whether they get divorced or use drugs. But now, as a parent, you do have control. You have control over how you raise your child. This is the time to decide that no matter how your parents choose (or don't choose) to support you and your baby, you have the power to make healthy choices and decisions for yourself. We'll talk about this more in chapter fourteen.

Stuck in the Middle—Being the Parent and the Kid

Once I had my baby, I felt like I didn't have to answer to anyone anymore. I had all this responsibility, basically no more fun. I was like, "Why do I have to put up with all of her nagging me about dishes in the sink and how I spend my money." My attitude did not go over that great with my mom. From her side, she felt like  helping me raise the baby brought even more work for her. She expected me to be even more helpful and respectful to her on account of what she was doing for the baby and me.

Allysa, 15 years old

One of the toughest things about raising a child with your mother is **being a mom and having a mom** at the same time, in the same place. Sometimes people have babies to prove that they're not kids anymore. You might feel like you don't need to follow your mom's rules now that you're a parent. But as long as you're living in her house, she has the right to decide curfews, who is in her house, and how much childcare she is willing to do. That doesn't mean that your voice doesn't matter. It does! But serious conflicts will probably come up if you don't respect the fact that it's her house.

We Know it Can Be Hard, But Be Open to Guidance and Help

My relationship was never very good with my mother. To be honest, I think I got pregnant on purpose. Actually, I know I did. I really wanted to have a baby because I wanted my family to stop treating me like a kid. Then once I had my daughter, I realized I didn't know what the hell I was doing. Then I needed my mom but felt too proud to ask her because I knew she was gonna be like, "I told you so." I thought it would prove that I really was just a stupid kid like they always said. But I really needed help, so I sucked it up and let her give me advice. At first it felt bad, like I failed, but now I see that there are some things she knows better about because she's been through it all before.

Jackie, 16 years old

It's okay to want to prove you can handle raising the baby on your own. And it's fine to want to be independent. But sometimes the wisest person knows his or her limits and lets others in to offer guidance, advice, and support. Allowing others to help can be especially hard if part of you had a baby to show that you are in charge of your life. Many young people have babies as a way to assert their independence. And you do have to be independent and strong to raise a baby. But being a parent isn't about proving things to people. It's about raising a healthy child. And for all parents, raising a child is a group effort. This is especially true if you are a young parent. Letting people teach you and help you doesn't mean you have failed. It means you really understand what it takes to be a parent.

And look, as long as you have a baby, someone's going to have advice for you. This is especially true if your mother is helping you raise your child. Trust us, she will have a lot of advice! Some of it will be great, some of it you might not be so sure of. Your job as a mother is to figure out the advice you're going to take. If you shut out the help and guidance your mom offers, you'll miss out on some ideas and information that could make your job a lot easier. On the other hand, there will probably be times when she gives advice that goes against how you want to discipline or teach your child. Our advice when it comes to raising your baby with your mom or anyone else is this: **Be open to suggestions and guidance, but think things through for yourself.**

Nice Move!

My mother and me have had a lot of problems since I got older, but she definitely knows how to take care of babies. She's real patient and gentle and I feel like she really is a good role model when it comes to taking care of children. Sometimes when the baby cries, I just get real stressed out and I want to scream and run out of the house. But then my mom takes him and starts rockin' him and humming in this soft low voice. It doesn't always work, but I can see that she's not stressed out and crazy like I felt. I hope that I can get to be more like her-calmer.

Diamond, 17 years old

✋ STOP AND THINK

If you are raising your child with your mother, family, or your partner's family, think about some of the positive things you have learned about parenting from them. Even if you don't like them, or have a lot of problems living with them, are there parenting tips or qualities (like patience, calmness, firmness, humor) that you have learned? If you feel like you haven't learned anything helpful, it's okay to write that down, too.

What I have learned from the people helping me raise my child:

Name of person:_____

What I have learned about being a parent:

1._____

2._____

3._____

Name of person:_____

What I have learned about being a parent:

1._____

2._____

3._____

Handling the Stress of Being a Mom with Your Mom

God, my mother and I get into fights worse than me and my son's father. It's horrible. It's like we're an old married couple. She yells at me about my son, always tellin' me to let him do things that she knows I don't want him doin'. Then I yell back and

say "No, he can't. I'm his mother and I say, 'no.'"
We go back and forth. Over and over again.

Carrie, 17 years old

Angela's Story

There was a lot of stress in Angela's house. She found out she was pregnant when she was fifteen. Her boyfriend said that he'd be there to help her, but he almost never comes around to give a hand or even see the baby. Angela's mother had to work two jobs to bring in enough money for the family that includes Angela, her eighteen-month-old baby, and Angela's three younger brothers and sister. Plus one of Angela's cousins has been living in the house since she lost her apartment. The place is crowded and noisy. Angela and the baby have to sleep in the living room, where the TV is. There are always arguments over when it goes on and how loud it will be. More than once a week, the TV wakes up Angela's baby and she has to get him calmed down and back to sleep.

Angela's mother needs her to help out with cooking, cleaning, shopping, and taking care of her brothers and sister while she is at work. Sometimes Angela feels like this is unfair, and she gets angry at her mom. Lately, when both of them are tired or stressed out, they scream at each other. The mood of the house has been getting more and more tense. Angela needs her mom to help her out so that she can finish school and try to find a job. A lot of time, Angela's mother can't help because she's at work or she's too tired to watch the baby after she gets home. Plus when she does take care of the baby, she does things that Angela doesn't want her to, like letting the baby sleep in her bed and letting him watch a lot of TV. Angela loves her mother, but she wants to move out and be more independent. She feels like she'd be less stressed out if she could do things her own way and have her own space. Her mom doesn't think Angela is ready to move out on her own yet and refuses to give her money for a deposit on an apartment.

 **STOP AND THINK**

What are some of the things causing stress between Angela and her mother? Can you think of any actions that Angela could take to help make the situation at home better? Now take a moment and think of some of the issues that cause stress between you and your mother (or anyone you are raising the baby with). Write them down in the space below. Now, think of two positive actions you could do to reduce the stress in your home. Write them in the space below. It could be anything that would make the situation better by using healthy or positive thoughts or behaviors. Brainstorm some solutions or steps you could take with other people whose opinion you value. This could be a counselor, teacher, or wise friend.

Stressful Situation #1: _____

_____

_____

Action Plan #1: _____

_____

_____

_____

Stressful Situation #2: _____

_____

_____

Action Plan #2: _____

_____

_____

_____

_____

Roadblocks and Disagreements

I love my mother and don't get me wrong, she helps me out a lot. And she's good with my daughter. But some of the stuff she says is the opposite of what I'm learning in my parenting class. She always gives in to the baby when she cries, but I know that my daughter uses that to get what she wants. So I tell my mother not to give in. Then I tell her why, like how it's going to make things even worse. I try to stay cool and not offend her, but sometimes she gets mad, like I don't appreciate what she does for us. But I really do. It's just that I have to make the choices that I feel are best for my daughter. I try to be respectful and everything, but I have to raise my daughter the way I think is right.

Gina, 17 years old

✋ STOP AND THINK

No two people agree on everything when it comes to raising a child. What are some of the issues that you and your mom don't agree on? It could be a disagreement over discipline. Maybe you *clash over whether the child should see his other parent or what the baby should eat. It could be how warmly to dress the baby or whether he should be allowed to cry himself to sleep. Write down the issues that you seem to clash over the most.*

My mom and I don't agree on _____

She wants to do it this way:_____

I want to do it this way: _____

On a scale of 1 to 10, rate how important this is to your

child's well-being:_____

Are you willing to compromise on this issue?

Yes or No _____

Talk So Your Mom Will Listen

Let's say you fill in the chart above and you write down an issue or a disagreement that you are not willing to bend on. Let's take spanking. When you were growing up, your mom hit you when you misbehaved. Well, you have been reading this book and you know that spanking is not the way to go. So you decide that you need to have a talk with her. If you start screaming and yelling, she'll probably tune you out or start screaming back at you. You need to talk so that she'll listen. Remember the Oreo exercise we showed you for your baby's other parent? Well, the same thing will work for your mother. Try it!

Take a moment and fill in the Oreo Chart below.

OREOs

Think back to a conflict that you have had with your mom about raising your child. Describe what happened and how you felt.

_____

_____

_____

_____

_____

Write down Cookie #1. It must be a true and believable thing about the other person that has something to do with the problem you are having. For example, if your mom spanked your son and you don't approve of spanking, you might say, "Mom, I know you care a lot about little James. And I really appreciate all that you do for us." _____

_____

_____

_____

_____

The Cream Filling. Using "I" statements, tell how you feel, what you want to have happen, and why this is a good thing for your child For example, "But I really don't believe in spanking. I've been reading this book and it says that spanking makes a kid act more aggressive and doesn't teach them anything about how you want them to act. I really want everybody to use time-outs instead. That way we're all on the same page, and he'll feel safer and learn faster." _____

_____
_____
_____
_____
_____

Cookie #2. Say another cookie, just to keep her listening and on track. It can be the same as cookie #1. For example, "Like I said, I know you only want little James to be happy and grow up right. He's lucky to have a grandma like you. I mean it!"

_____
_____
_____
_____
_____

COOKIES DON'T COME EASY! Giving cookies doesn't always feel normal or natural, but they work! Giving cookies isn't being a suck up or fake. It's good communication to get what you need.

Practice this with a friend so that it's ready to go next time a conflict pops up.

When Your Mom Wasn't
So Great of a Mom

When I was growing up, I didn't have anyone to support me or take the time to teach me about the world. Lately I been thinking about why my mom didn't get mad when I told her that I was pregnant. I think it was because she kind of blamed herself for it. She was never there for me to protect me and show me the way. I try not to hold it against her and throw it in her face about what a bad mother she was. Because she's trying to do better now. She helps me out with babysitting and buys the kids things. But when she tell me all the things I do wrong as a mother, I just want to scream at her that she's the last person who should be handing out advice.

Alexis, 22 years old

All moms make mistakes. There's no way around it. Being a parent is the toughest job in the world—and no one does it perfectly. But sometimes parents really screw up. Maybe your mom wasn't there for you. Maybe she was dealing with drug or alcohol addiction. Maybe she put the men in her life before you. Maybe she was so depressed, angry, or fearful that she couldn't take care of you the way you wanted or needed. It's sad when we miss out on parts of our childhoods because our parents aren't physically or emotionally there for us. You have the right to feel angry, disappointed, or any way else that you want.

But if your mom has turned her life around and wants to help you now, it might be time to leave behind the anger you have about the past to make way for your baby's future. That doesn't mean you can't express your feelings about the past to your mom. If that seems important for you to move on, it might be the right thing to do. (Just remember to use "I" statements. For example, "I felt sad and hurt when you left us with Grandma for two years while you had another baby.") Plus, it's also okay to ask your mom not to criticize your mothering skills. Nobody needs that! But letting go of resentment and disappointment from the past frees you to focus on the present. Sometimes people really do change. A lot of people who weren't great moms want a chance to make things right by being great grandmothers. The more help you receive and the more love your baby gets, the better for everyone!

Being Grateful

There's so much work to do when it comes to raising a baby. You might feel like you're carrying the whole load yourself. But if someone in your family is helping you raise your child, even a little, it's important to show them gratitude. Gratitude just means showing thanks for the support and help they give. It's great if our mothers are there to help us out. But their help is a gift, not a given. Any support we receive from our mothers or families should be valued and appreciated. It's important for you to be grateful for the times she takes care of the baby, does laundry for you, gives you money for formula, or cooks for you. Plus, showing gratitude has a funny way of making people want to do more for us.

STOP AND THINK

If someone in your family is helping you, take some time to write a letter of gratitude to them. List all of the things they do for you and your baby. Write down all of the ways your life would be different if you didn't have that person in your life. Tell them how their support makes you feel. Send this letter if it feels right. Or take a moment out of your day to say these things. You'll both feel glad you did!

Chapter 10

Hey Grandma (or Grandpa), This One's for You!

First, let us congratulate you on becoming a grandparent. Like we said in chapter ten, babies often offer us a fresh start or a new way of relating to the people in our family. Second, let us congratulate you for helping your child raise her child. You are probably making many sacrifices to take on this job. But there is no more important job in the world. This chapter is written for grandmothers (or anyone else) who are helping a young mom or dad raise a child. Your role is a powerful one. You have the potential to support your child emotionally, build his or her confidence as a parent, pass down child-rearing wisdom, and help him or her grow into an independent adult. Young parents who have parents of their own helping and guiding them are much more likely to be successful than those who don't. Your love and support are lifelong gifts to your child and grandchild.

Who's the Mother?

You might have very mixed feelings about your son's or daughter's parenthood. This is especially true if your child is young, still in school, or not in a stable relationship with the other parent. You might question whether your child is ready to take on the huge responsibility of raising a child. In truth, most teenagers are not ready to parent alone. And that's where you come in. The more support and guidance you can give your daughter or son to parent independently, the better off everyone will be. This means letting her assume the main responsibility of mothering. This can be tricky, especially if she is young or seems to be struggling with the role of mothering, but it's very important.

We like to think of raising a baby like making a movie. In a movie, there are stars and there is the supporting cast. While our attention is first drawn to the people who are the main characters, what would happen if all the other people weren't there? Obviously, there would be no movie. Without the supporting cast, the stars couldn't carry the weight of the film. In a way, the same thing happens when a young person becomes a parent. All the attention might be on them, but behind the scenes, the supporting characters (you!) have to be working and contributing to make sure the whole thing (raising the baby) is successful.

See how you rate as a supporting cast member. Try taking this grandma quiz before reading the rest of the chapter.

The Grandma Quiz

1) When my daughter is having a hard time with the baby (child won't sleep, feeding problems), I

    a) take the baby away from her and show her how it's done.
    b) ask her what she has tried and see if she wants my help.
    c) leave the room. It's her baby; she needs to figure it out.

2) When my daughter and I don't agree on a parenting choice (how to put the baby to bed, how warmly she should be dressed, how to discipline), I

    a) tell her to do it my way. I have a lot more experience and she should use it.
    b) ask her why she wants to do it that way and listen to what she says. If I strongly disagree, I try to explain why I think another way is better.
    c) never put my two cents in.

3) It is not unusual for babies and young children to prefer the person taking care of them the most. Let's say you are taking care of the baby a lot and he always seems to want to go to you instead of his mother. This hurts your daughter's feelings. You

    a) tell her that you do most of the work, so what did she expect.
    b) explain to her that the baby loves her, too, but babies like routines. He's just used to you taking care of him, but that doesn't mean he doesn't want his mother's attention and love, too.
    c) tell her it's no big deal. Forget it.

4) Your daughter's boyfriend (and father of the baby) wants to be involved. You don't really like the guy because he cheated on your daughter and lies to her a lot. But he's okay with the baby. Your daughter doesn't know what she should do. You

a) tell her she shouldn't let the father around the baby.

b) help your daughter figure out what's best for the baby and her. Talk to her about the positives and negatives of having the baby's father involved.

c) do nothing. It's her business, not yours.

How'd You Score?

If you picked **b** for every response, you are a great supporting cast member! Go back through and read the **b** responses again. All of these answers show that you respect your daughter's role as the primary caretaker. You listen to her opinions as a parent, but offer your own advice and personal experiences, especially around issues that involve the baby's safety. If you selected a lot of **a** answers, you might be trying to take the starring role! Although sometimes our children need extra support or guidance, it's important that everyone is clear who the mother is…the lead actor. If you answered a lot of **c**'s, you might have too much of a hands-off role. Remember, your daughter most likely needs and wants your guidance and expertise. Your job is to offer the support she needs until she is ready to become more independent. Don't leave her hanging! For the next few sections of this chapter, we're going to talk a little about why people fall into the **a** and **c** categories.

A Second Chance

When we run our groups for young mothers, we hear a lot of people say that their mothers were happy when they got pregnant. A lot of women are excited to become grandmothers. And that makes sense. Being a grandparent can be a wonderful experience. But sometimes people think that they want to become grandmothers, when really they want a second chance to be a mother. Let's say that you weren't exactly the kind of mom you hoped to be to your daughter. Maybe you had her really young and weren't ready for the responsibility, maybe you had other issues going on in your life that kept you from being the kind of mother you knew you could be. Perhaps you're older now, more mature, and more stable. In the back of your mind, you might see your grandchild as a chance to do it all over, but this time do it right. And it can be!

But it is really important to remember that this time you are doing it as a grandmother. And that means that your most important role is to help your child become an independent and healthy parent. If she doesn't feel like she is competent or able to take care of the baby, her attachment to her child will not be as strong. In the end, this hurts both the mother and the child. Sometimes grandmothers who are looking for a second chance push their daughters out of the way without really knowing they're doing it. If you answered **a** to a lot of the questions above, ask in the most gentle but honest way possible, is this you? Like we said, if you are a very involved grandparent, your daughter is so very fortunate. Just make sure that everyone is clear who the real mother is.

Of course, if your daughter is simply unable or unwilling to care for her child, then things are different. At that point, in a sense, you do take on the mothering role. However, we strongly urge you to keep open the possibility of letting your daughter assume the role whenever she is ready.

This is Your Mess...

To many people, news that your teenage daughter is pregnant is shocking and overwhelming. Anyone who has raised children knows the incredible personal sacrifice, time, energy, and money it takes. Imagining your fifteen-, sixteen-, or even twenty-year-old trying to do this can bring up well-grounded fears and concerns. Be patient with yourself. These feelings are natural. Your frustration may increase if you feel strongly that your daughter should end the pregnancy or consider adoption, but she decided to keep the child. When conflicts over significant life events occur, strong negative feelings often come up. These feelings tend to change over time, particularly after the birth of the baby. But many grandparents who feel as though their children disregarded their advice and opinions hold onto their anger. You might even have an "I told you so" attitude if you see your child struggling with parenthood.

Sometimes you may notice your teenager making choices without appreciation for the consequences of those actions. This isn't just your teenager being irresponsible; it actually has to do with the way the brain develops. Believe it or not, the human brain does not fully develop the parts responsible for planning and understanding the consequences of our behaviors until we are in our mid-twenties! That means that when teenagers make the decision to become parents, they may have very little idea of what that actually means. And most likely no amount of explaining can really drive home to a pregnant sixteen-year-old how radically her life is about to change. We are not suggesting that you don't try talking, reasoning, and explaining the realities of parenthood (especially before they get pregnant!), but don't be surprised if your words fall on deaf ears.

If you answered **c** to a lot of the responses in the quiz above, your anger and frustration over your child's pregnancy may be causing you to hold back on the support and help she needs. To some people, having their child fail or struggle is a way to prove that they were right. But at some point, if you are to help your child continue to grow and raise a healthy child herself, you will have to move beyond your anger and disappointment. Children grow fast. A year spent angry is a lifetime to a baby. And research tells us that a child's early years are the most important. You have a lot to offer. If your daughter or son needs your help, don't wait!

The Baby's Other Parent

You might not be happy about your daughter's choice to have a baby. But you might be even more upset because of who she had the baby with! It's not unusual for conflicts between teenagers and their parents to focus on the teen's choice of a boyfriend or girl-friend. To her, he might look like Prince Charming. But you see an immature boy focused on having a good time without really under-standing how his behavior affects those around him. She may love him just as much as you wished he never walked through the door. The whole thing gets even more complicated when that young man is linked to your lives forever with the birth of a child.

In an ideal world, all young men would be involved in their chil-dren's lives. But the truth is that most babies born to young moth-ers are raised by the mother and often, the grandmother. Many young men don't want to be burdened with the responsibility of raising a baby. But some young fathers are willing to step up to the plate and be involved in their child's life. If this is the case, your grandchild is very fortunate. And you, as the grandparent, are in a position of great power. The messages you send will be strong pre-dictors of whether that young man will feel welcomed or driven out. Really, it's just a choice you make. You can choose to put aside your dislikes and opinions and help that young man create an attachment to his child. Or you can push him away forever. Of course, if the young man doesn't want anything to do with being a father, there's probably nothing you can do to change his mind. But what about a teenager who shows some interest or one who is on the fence? That young man's involvement might be highly influenced by the way that you either welcome or shun him.

Special Note: If the baby's other parent is dangerous (a drug or alcohol abuser, has a history of physically abusing your daughter, or is involved in other very high-risk behaviors), you might be wise to limit his involvement with your grandchild. At the very least, his (or her) visitations should be supervised. But a lot of the time, the baby's other parent poses more irritation to us as parents than a threat to our grandchildren. No matter how immature or unreliable this person is, he (or she) is your grandchild's other parent. And he will be for life. Without fully realizing what we are doing, many of us send a loud clear signal to the baby's father—You're not wanted here. And many young men take this message seriously. They stop being involved in their babies' lives. Although this might feel good in the short run, in the long run it means that the child will grow up without a father. And that is almost never a good thing. Unless the parent is emotionally or physically abusive, kids do better and feel better when both parents are involved in their lives.

STOP AND THINK

If you have very strong negative feelings toward the baby's other parent, take a moment and reflect on some of these feelings. What thoughts or beliefs do you have about this person? In as gentle but honest a way as possible, ask yourself whether these thoughts and feelings cause you to push the baby's father (or mother) away from the baby? What, if anything, do you do to involve the father in his baby's life? When you think of the future, do you see the baby's other parent involved in the baby's life? What benefits do you think a relationship with both parents would bring to the child?

Laura's Story

Laura had her first child when she was sixteen. The father was an emotionally and physically abusive man who was almost twenty years older than her. He controlled how much money Laura was allowed, kept her away from her family and friends, cheated on her, and got her hooked on drugs. Within five years, Laura had three more children with other men and they were all taken away from her. Her life was a mess and she spiraled downward until she hit rock bottom. She was in a shelter, had no real friends, and missed her children so much she felt numb to the world. In the shelter she decided that the first step to getting her life back was to get clean. Laura started the path to recovery. After eight months, she tracked down her children and began visitation with them. This went on for a long time until she was able to get a job, find an apartment, and get her life back together.

After a few years, all of Laura's children were living in her house. Things weren't always easy, but she knew she was doing the right thing and felt proud of the progress she had made. She kept a steady job as a secretary and spent the rest of her hours trying to make up for lost time with her children. Then one day her fifteen-year-old daughter, Susan, came home and told her that she was pregnant and wanted to keep the baby. Laura was devastated and blamed herself for the pregnancy. She felt if she had been a better mother when the kids were younger, this wouldn't have happened. Laura felt disappointed that her daughter followed in her footsteps and became a mother so young. But in a way, it didn't surprise her. Susan was very angry at Laura for the past, and she reminded Laura of herself when she was that age. The difference was that while Laura didn't have a mother she could turn to when she found out that she was pregnant, Susan did. Laura expressed her beliefs that her daughter was too young to have a child, but respected Susan's decision to have the baby.

Laura helped Susan with the baby as much as possible. Together they were able to provide a loving and secure home for Jonathan. Laura encouraged Susan to continue school and find a career. By helping her daughter and grandson, Laura felt like she was making up for the mistakes of her past. She was able to help provide Jonathan with the kind of stable early childhood that her own children had missed. When she thought of his future, she felt hopeful that he would finish school, have a good job, and not go through the separations and disappointments her children experienced.

 **STOP AND THINK**

What are some of the benefits that Laura got from helping her daughter and grandchild? What are some of the benefits that Susan and Jonathan received from Laura's involvement? What made Laura a more effective grandmother than she was a mother?

Think about your own child's and grandchild's future. What do you hope to see for both of them? Going to school? Having stable and productive lives? Making friends and being part of a community? Think about the ways that you can contribute to making this vision happen. What are some of the day-to-day ways that you can help your daughter and your grandchild have a healthy future?

Chapter 11

Helping Your Child Handle Feelings

Sometimes I get swallowed up by my feelings—mostly the tough ones like anger and sadness. In my house we never did much talking about feelings. People just flipped out a lot when they was angry-screaming, hitting each other, and storming out of the house-staying away for hours or days. I had a lot of feelings I kept bottled up inside me that I never let out. I think that's why I did some of the messed-up things I did. But I know now that it ain't healthy. And I want my daughter to be able to come to me with how she's feeling. I want to teach her how to deal with her feelings so she doesn't lose control over every little thing.

Stephanie, 16 years old

Showing Respect is Teaching Respect

Ever heard of The Golden Rule? It just means treating people the way we want to be treated. One of the feelings all humans want to experience is respect. And the truth we all know deep down is: to get respect, you have to give respect. If you show your child respect, she'll grow up learning to treat herself and others the same way. We learn what we see. Teaching respect and giving respect are the first moves in getting a game plan together to teach your child how to handle his feelings successfully. Here are what the people at Healthy Families San Angelo suggest when it comes to teaching your child respect:

Respect her body: Don't wrestle with, tickle, pinch, hug, or kiss your daughter when she doesn't want you to. Don't make her hold your hand (unless crossing the street or in other situations that could be dangerous), sit in your lap, or hug and kiss people if she doesn't want to.

Respect his feelings: When your child is upset and crying, telling him to stop is the same as telling him he's not allowed to feel sad. Instead you might say, "You must be very sad about that." Whether he's happy, scared, angry or sad, he needs to know that it's okay to show his feelings.

Respect his thoughts and ideas: Even if you don't agree with what your toddler thinks, always listen to what he has to say. Talk about a lot of different things, and let him have his own opinions.

If you don't agree with him, say, "That's interesting. I never thought of that before." This shows him that what he thinks is important.

Respect her choices: Letting your child make her own choices as much as possible tells her that you believe she's smart enough to do things on her own. Let her know it's okay for her to make choices—and mistakes—sometimes. It makes her feel good about herself.

Respect her privacy: Let her know that people—both grown-ups and kids—have a right to do some things by themselves like going to the bathroom or changing clothes. If you respect her privacy, she will learn to respect her body…and other people's privacy. That will make it easier when you teach her about "safe" and "unsafe" touches.

(Healthy Families San Angelo, 1992)

 **STOP AND THINK**

Think of a time when someone really respected your feelings. Maybe this person listened carefully to what you were saying, tried to put himself in your shoes, or didn't judge you. How did that make you feel about the situation? Now think of a time when your feelings were disrespected, ignored, or you were shamed for feeling a certain way. Maybe you were told you "shouldn't" feel the way you did. How did that make you feel? Now ask yourself, "How do I want my child to feel when she expresses her feelings to me?"

Learning About Feelings

Why does this book spend so much time talking about teaching feelings to your children? Seriously, what's the big deal? Here are a few really good reasons to help your child become what we call "feelings smart"…

- Dealing effectively with your child's feelings can prevent temper tantrums!

- Kids who can manage their feelings do better in school because they can think more clearly.

- They will develop healthier friendships with teachers and friends.

- Children who manage their emotions fight less, are less likely to use violence, and get in less trouble.

- They grow up to be less anxious, worried, frightened, and depressed.

- They are better problem solvers.

- They are more successful and lead happier lives.

It may seem strange that teaching your child about his or her feelings can do all this, but, it can. Basically, becoming "feelings smart" means understanding and handling feelings so they don't rule us. It's knowing what we're feeling, why we're feeling it, and how to deal with those feelings in healthy ways. And guess who the biggest teachers are when it comes to being feelings smart? That's right, parents. Learning how to deal with feelings is like basketball or singing—to get good you need a coach—someone to give you tips and help you master the game. The rest of this chapter lays out all the information you'll need to take on your new role as your child's "feelings coach."

 **STOP AND THINK**

Before you read any more of this chapter, stop and think about the ways that your family members deal with their feelings. Think of your mother or the person who took care of you the most. How did she handle her fear? Her anger? Her worry or anxiety? Did she

express joy or excitement easily? Was she sad or stressed out a lot? What did she teach you about the way you expressed your feelings? Were you supposed to ignore them or pretend they didn't exist? Were you free to express feelings however you wanted? Did you feel like your parents accepted your feelings most of the time? Did your parents coach you on how to handle your feelings? Now, name one way you want to help your baby deal with her feelings differently than your parents did.

Feelings 411

Before we start, here is some basic feelings information.

Babies and kids have the same basic feelings as we do.

Babies don't have the same self-control. Our job is to teach this to them.

Your baby doesn't have the language to express how she's feeling. Our job is to help her learn the words that go along with her emotions.

NO FEELING LASTS FOREVER!

No feeling is wrong or bad, but it's important your child learns safe ways to express her feelings. Anger is okay. Hitting is not.

Never deny your child's feelings or shame him for what he feels.

Here are some examples of what to avoid…

Child: "I'm tired."
Parent: "You can't be—you just had a nap."

Child: (crying because he lost his balloon)

Parent: "That's ridiculous to get so upset over a little thing like that."

Child: "I hate ketchup."

Parent: "No you don't. Everyone likes ketchup."

Child: (scared of a barking dog)

Parent: "Don't be such a scaredy cat! He won't hurt you."

Baby's Feelings

The most important part of your coaching job at this age is to be sensitive. Because babies can't talk, you have to read her body signs to know what's going on. When your baby is a newborn (0 - 3 months), your emotional coaching job is to help her eat and sleep and to keep her from getting overstimulated. That means protecting her from too much noise, light, and touching.

As your baby gets older, from 3 to 12 months, your emotional coaching job still requires reading her signs and showing her you know how she feels (this is called empathy). If she's scared, hold her closely. If she's hungry, feed her. If she's fussy, comfort her. If she's alert and curious, play with her. During this age, you'll find that communication becomes a two-way street. Now she'll be reading and communicating with you, too, through her facial expressions, sounds, body movements, and even words.

Coaching Toddlers and Older Kids

There are some proven ways to help your child deal with his or her feelings. Here is what the experts say.

Like we said earlier, all children need to have their feelings RESPECTED

1) Be a good listener. Simply hearing what your child is feeling can calm him. Don't rush to fix things. Don't give advice. Don't argue. Just listen quietly and accept what he says.

To really get the idea of how powerful listening can be, try this exercise.

Imagine you come home from school angry and frustrated. Earlier, you had to take your child to daycare. The teacher kept you to discuss a serious issue about your child and you missed your bus. You were late for work and your boss was really angry and threatened to fire you. You tried to explain, but she wouldn't listen. The rest of the day didn't get any better. A friend blabbed a secret you asked her not to share. By the time you get home, you're in a really bad mood. Now imagine telling your mom or another adult what happened and she yells, "I've told you a hundred times you need to plan better. If you lose that job you are in a big mess!"

How would you feel?

_____

_____

_____

_____

Now imagine you come home and your parent sees right away you're unhappy. She asks what happened. You tell her. Instead of screaming she says, "Sounds like a really frustrating day." Or, "You're dealing with a lot right now. It sounds like you're being pulled in a lot of directions." She tries to see things from your side. Instead of judging, arguing, or accusing she just listens. She tries to "get it."

How do you feel now?

_____

_____

_____

_____

2) Acknowledging feelings only takes a word.

Instead of talking on and on, try some of these lines when listening to your child. Believe it or not, sometimes less is more. Examples....

I see

Hmmmm

Okay

I understand

Any short phrase that tells your child he has your full attention will work. Remember, it needs to feel genuine.

3) Name that feeling.

As your child describes what happened to him or her, label the feeling. This teaches her to connect feelings to words. Here are some examples.

That must have been **frustrating**.

Boy, you sound **really angry!**

Having your best friend move away probably made you feel **sad**.

I bet missing recess made you feel really **disappointed**.

4) Give your child his wish in fantasy.

As parents, we can't fix everything, but using fantasy to "magically" solve your child's problems makes him understand you "get it." Plus, it lightens the mood and can help avoid tantrums! Check out the following examples:

The pool is closed right now, but I wish I could use my magic wand to put one right in the backyard. Then we could both dive in!

Oh man, we're out of apples! Wouldn't it be great if we could use our super powers to turn all the bananas we have into delicious red apples!

(Faber and Mazlish, 1980)

My counselor told me that it was important to teach my baby about her feelings, like to label them and talk about them. At first it felt weird, but I see that it's working. She knows way more words about her feelings than the other kids in daycare. The other day when someone snatched a toy, she told the teacher she felt "angry inside." The teacher said how impressed she was and it made me feel proud, because I taught her that. Like the other day at the park, when someone ran up and got the swing right before her I could tell by the look on her face that she was gonna cry. When I was a kid my mother would have said something like "change that face before I change it for you." But that never worked and it made me just madder. So instead, I said, "Did that make you sad that you didn't get to go on the swing first?" The most important thing I learned to do was just to listen to her. I can tell it really takes a load off her.

Alexis, 22 years old

Ever Know There Were So Many Words for Feelings?

Pleasant Feelings

kind	happy	alive	good
understanding	great	playful	calm
confident	elated	courageous	peaceful
reliable	joyous	energetic	at ease
easy	lucky	warm	comfortable
amazed	fortunate	optimistic	pleased
free	delighted	hopeful	encouraged
sympathetic	overjoyed	admiration	clever
interested	gleeful	loved	surprised
satisfied	thankful	secure	content
sure	determined	quiet	certain
accepting	festive	spirited	relaxed
comforted	ecstatic	thrilled	serene
loving	satisfied	wonderful	reassured
considerate	glad	fascinated	bright
affectionate	cheerful	inspired	blessed
sensitive	sunny	passionate	strong
tender	close	inquisitive	enthusiastic
devoted	curious	touched	brave
attracted	positive	eager	bold
excited	earnest		

Difficult or Unpleasant feelings

angry	depressed	confused	helpless
irritated	lousy	upset	incapable
enraged	disappointed	doubtful	alone
hostile	discouraged	uncertain	paralyzed
insulted	ashamed	indecisive	fatigued
sore	powerless	perplexed	useless
annoyed	diminished	embarrassed	inferior
upset	guilty	hesitant	vulnerable
hateful	dissatisfied	shy	empty
unpleasant	miserable	stupefied	forced
indignant	despicable	skeptical	hesitant
bitter	disgusting	distrustful	despair
aggressive	terrible	tense	frustrated
resentful	in despair	lost	distressed
inflamed	sulky	unsure	woeful
provoked	bad	uneasy	pathetic
incensed	a sense of loss	pessimistic	tragic
infuriated	anxious	afraid	wary
cross	fearful	nervous	scared
fuming	cold	terrified	worried
disinterested	weary	suspicious	frightened
insensitive	bored	anxious	timid
dull	preoccupied	alarmed	rejected
menaced	sad	concerned	injured
restless	tearful	unhappy	offended
doubtful	sorrowful	lonely	alienated
threatened	pained	grieved	wronged
cowardly	grief	mournful	victimized
hurt	desolate	dismayed	heartbroken
humiliated	desperate	pained	agonized
appalled	tortured	dejected	challenged
deprived	impulsive	rebellious	

(Adapted from www.psychpage.com)

More Than Sad, Mad, and Glad

Take another look at the list of feelings. There are a lot of them, right? We've already said that being a feelings coach involves teaching her the right word for her feeling. For example, Susan gets a call from her friend. They were supposed to go to the mall to get some new clothes. Her friend has to work and can't go. Sue tells her mother that she's mad. But what might be a more exact word for how she's feeling? How about disappointed, or let down? Maybe she feels irritated or even annoyed if this happens all the time? The point is, if you only teach your child sad, mad, and glad, that's all he'll know. Every time something irritating happens he might label that feeling as "mad," when really he's feeling disappointed, frustrated, or annoyed. The more feelings words your child knows, the more feelings smart he'll be!

Look at the feelings list. Circle all of the words that you use regularly. Challenge yourself and see how many new words you can work into your own vocabulary!

Teaching Tip: When you read to your child, point to the different characters in the pictures and ask him how each of the people in the story is feeling. Ask your child how he would feel if the same thing happened to him. Use the feelings list to teach your baby new feeling words.

Dealing with Strong Feelings (Especially Anger)

My son has been in a bad mood for the past two weeks. He wakes up pissed off at the world and starts beatin' on his sisters and yellin' at me. He's only three and he's been swearing at school and losing control of himself when he gets angry. The teachers say that he won't be able to go to that school if he doesn't get his temper under control. I know that my boyfriend and me have problems with our anger and don't always keep our cool. I don't know what to do with him. Sometimes when he gets angry and starts flippin' out, I just start screaming at him. I know that probably doesn't help, but I don't know what to do. Can you give me some ideas?

Christine, 17 years old

Anger is a part of life. We all feel it from time to time. For some of us, anger might even be a problem. A big problem. **Getting control of your anger** is the number one most important thing you can do to help your child express her anger in a healthy way. It's simple. How you manage your anger has a lot to do with how your child will deal with her anger. **We learn what we see.** If your child sees the people around her flying off the handle over the smallest frustration, chances are she'll do the same. On the other hand, if she sees a person who gets angry, acknowledges his anger, and expresses his anger safely, most likely she will learn these skills too.

I think I was born mad. Mad at the world for having shitty parents, mad at the people in my life who hurt me. Just mad at everything, all the time. If you pissed me off in the morning, I'd be pissed off until my head hit the pillow at night. In a way, I think my anger worked for me sometimes because it made people afraid of me. It kept people from getting in my face and messing with me. But now that I have a daughter, I don't want to be this way anymore. I don't want to go around angry at the world. I don't want her to learn this from me. My mother was like that and I think she kind of passed it on. I don't want to do that to my daughter. I don't want her to grow up feeling so much hate and anger.

Erin, 19 years old

I wonder about my anger sometimes. Where did it come from? I start yelling at the slightest little thing. My parents did that, too. I explode at things and don't even know how it happened. I wonder how I would be if my parents weren't the way they were with their tempers and anger. Then I wonder. . . what am I teaching my daughter? Am I putting my anger on her just like my parents did to me?

Susan, 17 years old

Take a minute and think about how you deal with anger. Do you yell? Pretend that you aren't mad when inside you're burning up? Do you find healthy ways to deal with your anger, like writing a letter to say how you feel? Taking some deep, calming breaths? Listening to relaxing music? Or going for a walk? How do other people in your family deal with their anger? What is your baby learning about anger from the other people in your family?

Think back to the last time you were angry. What triggered your anger? Describe how you handled those angry feelings.

_____

_____

_____

_____

Drama Ain't for Mamas

Are you addicted to drama? When you watch daytime television and see people screaming or throwing chairs at each other, do you think they're just "expressing" themselves? Do you thrive on tension and conflict in relationships? When people are just getting along, do you find it boring? Does trouble follow you? If you answered yes to any of these questions, you might be a drama junkie. Lots of young people are drama junkies. It's a rush or a thrill. They stir the pot and cause trouble because they like the excitement or it makes them feel important. But here's the truth: BABIES DON'T LIKE DRAMA! They hate it. Why? Because what goes along with drama? Stress, tension, yelling, dirty looks, sometimes physical fighting, anger, and resentment. All of these things make babies feel uncomfortable, frightened, unsafe, and confused. And don't fool yourself into thinking the baby isn't picking up on what's going on. Because he is! If you find yourself drawn to drama with friends or boyfriends/girlfriends, you need to drop the drama. Just walk away. If you can't do it for yourself, do it for your baby!

Next time you feel like you're going to snap, remember the ABCs of keeping cool.

A lways pause—before you do *anything*.

B reathe—until your body is calmer
and your mind is clearer.

C onsider the consequences of your actions.
Choose carefully.

And remember, someone's watching everything you do!

Babies and Anger

Even young babies feel angry. Usually it starts with frustration over something not going the way they want. Pretty soon it grows into full-blown anger. So what do you do? Well, the first thing to remember is it's okay for your baby to get frustrated for short amounts of time. In fact, frustration motivates him to learn and act. He's frustrated that he can't reach a toy, so he tries harder to crawl so he can get it. Over time he'll learn how to control his frustration.

Here are some tips on how to help your baby with her frustration and anger.

Help your baby connect his feelings with words. If he's screaming his head off because you won't give him the pair of scissors, say to him, "I can see that you are very mad that I won't give those to you. But they are not toys. How about these keys?"

Know your baby's limits. If your baby is tired or hungry, soothe her rather than let her be frustrated. You are the expert on your child. You know when she's reached the end of her rope.

It's okay for your baby to see you get angry. This shows him that anger is natural and we all feel it. You can even tell him how you feel. "I am so frustrated that we brought our clothes to the laundro-mat and it's closed. That makes Mommy feel really cross."

It's very important not to lose control in front of your baby, no matter how angry you are. Seeing you lose control is incredibly scary for your child. It makes her feel unsafe.

REMEMBER! Angry feelings are okay, but violent or destructive actions are not. It is important to help your child separate feelings from behavior. Just because he feels angry doesn't mean he has the right to hit or break things. As a parent, it is important to put safe limits on how your child expresses his anger (or any feeling). Read the example below. Notice how the parent listened to how her child was feeling and also put limits on his behavior.

> **Mom:** That made you really angry when your sister broke your new toy.
>
> **Child:** I hate her. I'm gonna break one of her toys to pay her back.
>
> **Mom:** I know how upset you are, but it's not okay for you to break something of hers. She touched something of yours without permission and she'll have consequences. But if you break something of hers on purpose, there will be consequences for you, too.
>
> **Child:** I loved that thing. I wanted it so bad. And now it's wrecked.
>
> **Mom:** That was your birthday present. That's got to be really disappointing. I'm really sorry.

Teaching Her How to Calm Down

Sometimes when I'm really heated, I throw things. Like the other day, I was having an argument with my boyfriend and I threw a book at him. It hit the wall and made a big dent. It let out a lot of steam for me. But then the other day I saw my son doing it. I totally freaked because I realized *that he must've got that from watching me. Now I'm trying to calm myself down in other ways. I take a few deep breaths until I feel more relaxed. Another thing is to call my sister who I'm tight with and tell her everything that happened to stress me out.*

Angela, 17 years old

Showing your child how to feel better when she's upset is very important. Babies and children need to learn how to calm themselves down when they are upset, stressed, or sad. It is called self-soothing, and it's something they'll need to know how to do for the rest of her life. Think about it. Do you know people who turn to drugs and alcohol to make themselves feel better when they are feeling down? Or people who always eat a lot when they're stressed? Do you know people who fight or act aggressively to get away from the bad feelings they have? Do you see any negative self-soothing going on in your family?

Take a minute to think about what you do to soothe yourself.

When I'm stressed I_____

When I'm sad I usually_____

When I'm frustrated I often_____

REMEMBER! Difficult feelings can't kill you! You're strong enough to sit through anger, sadness, or jealously. Sometimes just accepting your feeling is the best way to deal!

Healthy Self-soothing

Here's a list of healthy ways to soothe yourself. Did we leave any out that work for you?

Talk to someone you're close to, get some fresh air, exercise, cook, watch a little television, meditate, write in a journal, draw, listen to music, get your frustration out by cleaning the house like crazy, go hang out at the park and push the baby on the swing, read this book!

Things That Soothe Babies

Think about your own child for a minute. What calms, relaxes, or soothes him? Is it being held? Having someone read to him? Being rocked by someone he loves? If your baby is young, does sucking on a pacifier or bottle relax him? Here are a few things that often soothe babies.

Having someone sing to him, taking a bath, going in a swing, a ride in the car or a stroller, being held or rocked, being shown a toy, sucking on fingers or a pacifier, any kind

of distraction, playing peek-a-boo, hearing gentle music

*I know that my baby is soothed by*_____

*Another thing that soothes my baby is*_____

Big Kids Need Soothing, Too!

It's not just babies who need practice self-soothing. All kids need to learn how to calm themselves down. As your child gets older, you'll be able to use words to help him soothe himself. Read what Gina said to her three-year-old who wanted to have the first turn pushing a toy stroller at the park, but an older cousin got there first.

I know you wanted to go first and you're probably feeling a little angry right now, but you'll get your turn real soon. Why don't we go over and play on the swings while Arielle takes her turn? Then when she's done, you'll get a turn. How does that sound?

Basically, by understanding your child's feelings and helping him manage those feelings, you're training him to be a calmer, more in-control person. It's like you're putting a recording in his head that he can use when he is stressed or things aren't going his way. You're teaching him to look on the bright side. You're teaching him to be effective. And effective people have a much easier life!

Now, take a minute and write down five things that soothe an older child. Ask yourself if there are any negative consequences for your answers. For example, what might happen if you teach your child to self-soothe by giving her cookies?

1._____

2._____

3._____

4._____

5._____

The Mood Matters

Not once that I can remember. Not once do I remember my mother smiling when I was a little kid. Everyone was always feeling stressed or angry or something. If us kids would laugh at the table or joke around, she would tell us to cut it out or slap us on the head. Even when we did somethin' good, she would just shake her head, but no smile, no happiness. It was just like there was always a black cloud hangin' over that house. I never wanted to go home because it was too damn depressing. Maybe that's why I kept getting locked up, so I didn't have to stay there.

Oa'Qwan, 18 years old

Did you ever have this feeling growing up? Like your house was a tomb or a war zone? If you're living with a parent or in someone's house, you may not be able to totally control whether it's a happy, relaxed place or one like Da'Qwan described. But you do have a say over how much happiness your baby sees from you. If you feel angry or stressed all the time, that is what your child grows up learning. *Laughing and playing with your child is just as important as feeding him. This is how he learns joy. Take time every day to lighten your child's mood by just goofing around.*

important Note on Feelings and Mood!

If you feel like you're sad all the time and can't shake it, you might need help. Or if you

- aren't feeling like yourself
- are sleeping too much or too little
- are eating more or less than usual
- feel on edge all the time
- are crying a lot

Or... if things that used to be fun don't give you any joy **you might be depressed.** It is very hard to take care of yourself or your child if you are depressed and you **MUST GET HELP.** A doctor, a school nurse, counselor, or a trusted adult are people you can ask for help. Depression is serious, and if you are depressed you will need some help to really deal with it.

Depression isn't good for you and it's really bad news for your baby to have a depressed parent. The sooner you get help, the sooner you'll start to feel better. Don't wait!

Chapter 12

Healthy Discipline

The hardest thing for me about being a parent is knowing how to discipline my son. I definitely don't want to do it how my parents did it. From as early as I can remember, my parents were always hitting us for something-even little things that all kids do. Not eating our dinner, saying "no" to them, having a dirty room. And you know what? It definitely did not work. So I'm not gonna do that with my baby. But then to tell you the truth, I'm not really that sure what I am supposed to be doing.

Latisha, 17 years old

If you grew up in a family where there was a lot of screaming and hitting, you might feel in your gut that there's a better way. But then the question is, How *do* you want to discipline your child? What's the most effective way? In this chapter we're going to pass along to you what the experts say. We'll break it down by the age of your child, because obviously you're not going to discipline an eight-month-old baby the same way you would a four-year-old.

At the beginning of each age group, we'll include a box of normal development facts. Sometimes if you know that most two-year-olds say "no" a lot (because they are learning to be independent), it won't rattle your cage so much. You'll be able to see it and maybe even laugh. Or at least say to yourself, "Oh yeah, that means he's developing just like he should." Knowing a little about child development helps you keep things in perspective and under control.

 **STOP AND THINK**

Think back to your own childhood. How were you disciplined as a young child? As a teenager? Do you think this style was effective? Do you choose to discipline the same way that your mother, father, or other caretaker did?

So What is Discipline?

According to the mega-experts (American Academy of Pediatrics), **Discipline is Love.** What do they mean by this? Well, by teaching her discipline, you're teaching her how to have self-control. People who have self-control usually don't get into lots of trouble. This means they tend to have more productive, better lives. People with self-control do better in school. They hold their jobs because they don't fly off the handle at their bosses and get fired.

They have better friendships, so they feel more satisfied.

Discipline also teaches children to act respectfully and honestly to those around them, which makes them more accepted and loved. **Discipline is not punishment or getting back at your child. Discipline is teaching.** Discipline is giving your child the tools she needs to deal with the world. And that is the best kind of love you can give.

Limit Setting

Children want to know that their worlds are safe and predictable. No matter how they might act, no child wants to feel like they can do whatever they want whenever they want. Because young children do not have self-control, your control over them is what keeps them safe. And it is how they learn to develop their own self-control. Part of being a loving and effective parent is figuring out the limits for your child. Here are a few things to keep in mind about limits.

> • **Different-aged children need different limits.** So the limits will change as your child grows older.
>
> • **For young children, limits should involve safety.** Keep the rules to a minimum. Too many rules are confusing. It makes it hard for the child to figure out which rules you really mean.
>
> • **Limit setting helps kids learn "right from wrong" and "good from bad."** These are very important lessons for all children, and they start early.
>
> • **Limits and rules should be consistent.** That means from day to day, the rules should be the same. Changing the rules quickly is confusing to your child.

• **When you are disciplining your child for breaking the limits, it should be immediate.** That means if your child needs a time-out for throwing sand, he should have it right then, not twenty minutes later. Children have limited memory for things that happen in the past. The best way to teach is to discipline your child immediately after he has broken a rule.

• **If at all possible, all people caring for the child should have the same limits and rules.** Talk to your parents and anyone else taking care of the child so that everyone is on the same page.

What's Your Real Role as a Parent?

I want to be my baby's best friend. I want to be the coolest parent ever and go places together with her and just hang out. I want my baby to love me, so I don't want to be nagging at her all the time like my parents always are to me. No, I'm definitely gonna be the mom who all the kids want to be around, 'cause I won't get on their case for all the little things.

Markesia, 15 years old

 **STOP AND THINK**

What do you think about what Markesia said? Why do you think she wants to be a cool mom? What are some of the parenting problems she might face by taking on a cool mom role?

Being a parent means that we can't always be the "good guy." It means making tough choices, laying down the rules in a loving way, and deciding for your child what's right. Don't worry that your baby won't love you if you don't give her what she wants all the time. It's your job to make those choices for her so that later she can make them for herself. A young child doesn't have their best interest in mind when it comes to choosing their bedtime, how much TV to watch, or what to eat. That's where you come in.

Letting your child do whatever he wants is trouble for a couple of reasons. First, it will make your life very hard, because you won't have control. Second, it will make your child feel unsafe. Kids need to know that there are boundaries and limits. Loving your two-year-old means saying no when he wants ice cream for dinner. It means buckling him in his car seat even when he fights it. It means shutting off your six-year-old's video game when he's had enough. It might not be what they want, but it's what they need. And your job as a parent is to figure out what they need and give it to them. **When we give them what they want all the time (and not what they need), that's spoiling. And nobody wins.**

Never Spank—Just (Don't) Do it

For a long time when my son would touch something he wasn't supposed to or if he hit me, I would hit him back. More like a tap. But I noticed that it didn't seem to stop him because in a little while he was right back at it again. And sometimes, like if he really did something bad, like throw something at me, I would really burn his butt. But then I noticed that he started hitting back and that really freaked me out because here was this little kid and we were practically in fist-fights. After I learned about how to give time-outs, I was shocked. They really changed some of the negative stuff he was doing. And I can tell you, hitting him never fixed anything.

Alexis, 22 years old

Hitting Your Child Doesn't Work

Hitting or spanking might stop your child from doing something that's annoying. But we know that it doesn't work in the long run. And it almost always causes harm either physically or emotionally. According to one study, kids who are hit grow up to feel more depressed and anxious. They feel less close to their parents. Here's our case against hitting…

• Spanking doesn't teach your child what he is supposed to be doing, so chances are it won't improve his behavior.

• Spanking shows him that it's okay to solve problems with violence.

• Spanking chips away at the trust that you've worked so hard to build with your child. In its worst forms, spanking can become physical abuse. When the person who is supposed to be caring for you and protecting you hits you, some children begin to confuse pain and love. This is very dangerous! It sets your child up to hurt or be hurt by others.

• Hitting can cause your child to feel angry and resentful toward you. This may cause him to act out even more. Believe it or not, some kids like the negative attention they get from a spanking. It may make them feel like they've really gotten through to you.

• In extreme cases, spanking or hitting your child can cause physical injury.

(American Academy of Pediatrics, 2004)

What's the Difference Between Abuse and Discipline?

For a long time I didn't even admit to myself that I was abused by my family. Part of me felt like I deserved what I got because I really did cause a lot of trouble. And it wasn't just the physical stuff like the hitting, slapping, and whatnot. We'd hear things all the time like how we were useless and that all the troubles of my family were because of us. When we did something wrong my dad would say that it was just more proof that we were morons or idiots. As I got older, watching how my friends were treated by their families, I knew it was messed up. I never want to put my kids through that. No way.

Erica, 19 years old

Abusive Behavior

Just so we're all on the same page, we want to be clear about the difference between abuse and discipline.

Physical abuse comes in the form of hitting, punching, kicking, burning, scratching, squeezing so hard that the child has a bruise, or any other act that could physically hurt the child.

Emotional abuse is using words or looks to make the child feel stupid, useless, scared, or in danger. Emotional abuse also includes leaving kids alone for long periods of time before they are ready or able to take care of themselves. Things like throwing out the child's clothes or toys as punishment is emotional abuse. Being treated worse than other children in the family is emotional abuse. When kids are not supported, loved, or cared for it is called neglect. And while it may not seem as bad as being hit or punched, it can cause just as much pain and suffering.

Sexual abuse happens anytime someone who is more powerful gets a child to engage in sexual behaviors. Even if the child agrees to the sexual behavior or enjoys it, it's still abuse! Sexual abuse can include kissing, touching sexual parts of the body, intercourse, or oral sex. Being shown pornography by someone older or more powerful or having someone make sexual comments is also abuse. **If you suspect your child is being abused—trust your gut.** If you think someone is unsafe or has a history of unsafe sexual behavior, don't let them be around your child alone. **If your child tells you that someone has been touching him or her in an unsafe way or in a way that "doesn't feel right," IT IS VERY IMPORTANT TO LISTEN TO HER OR HIM AND TAKE ACTION TO PROTECT HER OR HIM. Not believing her or him is just as emotionally damaging as the abuse itself.**

Safe Touch

Another way to keep your child safe from sexual abuse is to teach her or him about **safe** and **unsafe** touch from a very young age.

Teach your child that certain parts of his or her body—like breasts, bottom, penis or vagina—are private, and no one else beside his or her doctor should touch them. Also, she or he has the right not to be touched in anyway that makes him or her feel uncomfortable (like kissed on the mouth). Let your child know that if anyone touches him or her in a way that feels unsafe or scary, he or she should come to you right away. **This should be taught to boys and girls.**

Sometimes young siblings or friends will touch each others' private parts out of curiosity. If you see this happen, stop the behavior and say, "Those are your private parts. No one else can touch them. That is unsafe touch and you have to stop." Don't shame them for their interest, but make it clear that it's not okay.

IT IS OKAY FOR YOUR CHILD TO TOUCH HIS OR HER OWN PRIVATE PARTS. This is part of normal development. Even babies do this, not because it's sexual, but because it soothes them and feels good. It is important not to shame them for exploring their body. When your child is old enough, you can teach him or her to do this in a private place.

Important note: If you were touched in a sexual way by caregivers (for example, had your genitals rubbed, were forced to lie naked with someone, had a caregiver or adult ask you to touch their genitals or breasts) it is very important that **you do not do this with your own child.** If you find this happening, stop the behavior right away. Your child's body belongs to him and he has the right to be safe and protected.

Hints and Help for Healthy Discipline

Up to 4 Months Old (No Discipline!)

At this age, babies don't need any kind of discipline at all. If she cries, comfort her. The most important thing at this age is that babies know that their cries of discomfort, fear, hunger, cold, or plain fussiness will be met with love and patience.

5 to 7 Months Old (Redirect)

The only time you may need to discipline your baby at this age is if he is doing something dangerous to himself or someone else. For example, you don't want him pulling the cat's tail because it is painful to the cat and may cause your child to get seriously hurt. At this stage, simply redirect your child to another activity—that means find him something else to do. Get a book and read to him or put some toys in front of him. This is the only discipline he needs at this age.

7 to 12 Months Old

Normal Development for Babies 7 to 12 Months Old

- Children this age love to explore by touching and tasting. This curiosity is how he learns. Expect him to grab every thing he can get his hands on!

- At this age she has very little self-control over her emotions and her actions. She will most likely get frustrated easily and needs your help to calm down.

- He still has a short memory and very little sense of time. Don't expect him to remember what happened even an hour earlier.

- Stranger anxiety and separation anxiety will begin during this time. Expect her to be clingy if she thinks you might be leaving. New people will probably frighten her.

- Don't expect your baby to share. It's okay to try and teach him about sharing, but his ability to do this on his own is still a way off. Your baby is still very self-centered and that's perfectly natural!

- Very young babies have no idea of the difference between "good" and "bad"—this takes a long time to develop.

Discipline for Babies 7 to 12 Months Old

No! By the time your baby is between seven or eight months old, you can teach him the word "no." But be careful not to overuse it or it won't mean anything. If a baby hears "no, no, no" all the time, how will he know when to take you seriously? Only use "no" for dangerous activities. Here's an example. You're outside and the baby starts to eat food off the ground. Instead of screaming "No!" just take it out of his hands and say, "This is dirty. It's for the birds." Then throw it away.

Distract him whenever possible. If he is trying to climb up a bookshelf, take him to another room or outside.

Never be harsh. Use a calm voice whenever you are disciplining. Take a few deep breaths if your child's behavior has made you angry.

Use the two-step method. If he's doing something that is unsafe like pulling his sister's hair try this:

1) *Tell him "no"* in a firm voice with a frown on your face.
2) *Redirect him* to a positive activity. For example, give him

something constructive he can do with his hands.

Reward positive behavior. If he stops whining and starts playing, tell him, "What a big boy you are to find a nice game." Give him a hug. This actually teaches him what to do instead of crying!

12 to 24 Months Old

Normal Development for 12 to 24 Month Olds

- Children at this age are very self-centered. They honestly think the world revolves around them! This is both normal and healthy.

- Don't expect your child to share yet. Keep practicing with him whenever the chance comes up. If a friend wants to see his toy, tell your son, "Yes, this is your toy, but John just wants to see it for a minute. That's okay, he'll give it back."

- Your child will want more independence from you. However, she's not as big as she sometimes acts. Chances are she'll go back and forth between seeming like she doesn't need you and clinging to your leg! Separation anxiety still makes her get scared when you leave.

- Expect to hear the word "no" a lot. Try not to overreact. It's just his way of trying to control his world.

- Toddlers will naturally discover their genitals and will touch them because it is pleasant. This is perfectly natural and all children do it. Don't worry yet about teaching him privacy. The time for that will come.

- Expect temper tantrums. Your child is still learning how to control her feelings. When she reaches her breaking point and gets upset or frustrated, chances are you'll see a tantrum.

Some aggressive behavior toward other kids is natural. Your toddler hasn't learned how to control his feelings yet, so when he's angry, he might hit. Plus, he still doesn't know that his kicking and scratching are causing pain to other people because he doesn't feel it.

Discipline for 12 to 24 Months Old

Ignore what you can. If your child has figured out that whining, kicking, and screaming will get your attention, she'll keep doing it. Ignoring negative behavior often makes it go away. Of course, never ignore dangerous behaviors of any kind. Those need your attention right away.

Remember, don't overload the rules. Think safety. Most rules at this age should be limits to keep her and others (pets, cousins, siblings) safe.

Keep your cool. There will be times when your toddler's behavior might make you go nuts. Try to have a sense of humor about it if you can.

Use the playpen (or crib) time-out. Let's say your child keeps hitting the cat (after you've said "no" several times and redirected him to other activities). You can then move on to the Playpen Time-out. Here's how it works.

1. Tell her **No** in a firm voice with a frown on your face.

2. Tell her **why** she's getting a time-out. "I am giving you a time-out because you hit the cat and that hurts her. It is not okay to hit the cat. I want you to play nicely with her and pat her like this." Model what you want her to do.

3. Put her in a playpen or crib for **one minute** (no longer). The playpen should be away from people, TV, and should have no toys.

4. After a minute go and pick her up with a smile on your face. And say in a warm voice, "Okay, let's go play."

Praise your baby when she does something positive. If she shares something, stops crying, or touches her sister gently, make a fuss about it. She wants to please you and will do these things to get your praise. If your baby only gets your full attention when she's naughty, guess what's going to happen!

2 to 3 Years Old

Normal Development for 2 to 3 Year Olds

- Your toddler is becoming even more independent. You may find she wants to do things "her way." She will probably "test the limits" quite a bit.

- She's still learning to express her emotions. Temper tantrums will happen when she gets frustrated. (Check out pages 198-203 on dealing with your child's tantrums.)

- To your toddler, the world still revolves around him. This does not make him a selfish or greedy person. It's how all children this age see the world. Respect his right not to have to share his special toys. And don't expect him to want to share any of his things. But if he does, praise him!

- Separation anxiety (when she doesn't want to be away from you) is still a factor. This may cause her to act clingy or be upset every time you try to leave her. Remember to comfort her. (See page 48 on dealing with separation anxiety.)

- Your three-year-old's language skills are growing every day, but they are still limited. Don't be surprised if she calls you names or even says she hates you when she becomes frustrated. She doesn't, but this is how she lets you know how she feels. Try not to overreact or get your feelings hurt.

- His imagination is in full swing. He may have trouble telling the difference between his "fantasy" life and "reality." It is important not to confuse storytelling and fantasy with "lying." Imaginary friends and make-believe adventures are common.

- Because she is becoming more aware of the world and her imagination is so active, she may develop new fears, like of the dark or of dogs. Talk to her about her fears. Reassure her that she is safe.

At this age, toddlers are into everything. They learn by exploring their world. Keep the word "no" to a minimum. If you're always stopping your child's investigations, he will feel like he has no control over himself and his world. And this is exactly what your child needs to be building at this age—a sense of mastery and independence.

Discipline for 2 to 3 Year Olds

Most of the discipline guidelines listed above still work for this age. Remember to **ignore** what you can, then **distract**, and **redirect** to other activities.

Reprimand. This means say "no" with a frown when she does something unacceptable (but not dangerous) like roughhousing, playing too loudly, playing ball in the house, or splashing water out of the tub. Reprimanding is for things that aren't so serious that they need a time-out, but that you want to stop. Here's how to do it:

1. *Tell her what to stop.* "Please do not splash water out of the tub."

2. *Tell her why to stop.* "It makes a big mess and it will ruin the ceiling downstairs."

3. *Tell her what to do instead.* "When you play, keep all the water inside the tub or I will make you get out."

4. *Praise her as soon as she does what you asked.* "Good job playing with your toys so the water stays in the tub! I'm so proud of you. I knew you could do it!"

(Kazdin, 2005)

Set reasonable limits for your child. Think about her developmental stage. For example, don't have breakable things lying around the house and expect your two-year-old not to touch them.

Be a role model for safe, decent, and kind behavior. If you treat people with respect, she'll learn to do the same. Learning takes many, many tries! Don't expect to teach your toddler something after just one time out. You might have to give her thirty or forty time-outs before she stops hitting the cat! Don't give up and think it's impossible after a couple of shots. Stick with it.

Keep using time-outs, but by the age of three, your child can be expected to sit on a chair in an empty room rather than in her playpen. But remember to keep time-outs to under two minutes. It might not seem like a long time to you, but to your child it might feel like forever.

Praise and reward good behavior. This teaches her the right things to do. Did you know that there's a way to praise that's most effective?
Here it is:

★ *Praise your child when you are near him. He'll pay better attention.*

★ *Use a genuine tone of voice. You don't have to be loud, but show that you're really excited.*

★ *Touch, hug, kiss, high-five, or pat her on the back while you praise. It helps the praise really sink in.*

★ *Tell your child exactly what you're praising him for. "Great job picking up your toys and putting them in the basket. That's a big help to me and I really appreciate it!"*

(Kazdin, 2005)

Try having everyone raising your child follow the same rules and use the same discipline. We know this is hard, and it's not always even possible, but do the best you can. It won't take her long to figure out how to "get by" on people if she thinks she can. Plus lots of different rules can be confusing to her.

3 to 5 Years Old

Normal Development for 3 to 5 Year Olds

- Your child now has more control over her feelings and behavior. But you can still expect an occasional meltdown especially if she's tired, hungry, or getting sick.

- His language is developing rapidly and he's now more able to use words to solve problems. Help him learn to do this by talking things through in detail, explaining situations, and encouraging him to express his feelings.

- Her fantasy life is very active. At times (especially around three years old) she may have trouble knowing the difference between fantasy and reality. Don't threaten her that you'll "lock her in the closet if she misbehaves" or "leave her on the street if she doesn't hurry up." She may actually believe you.

- During this age, he will develop an interest in his and other people's bodies and how they work. Give him honest, accurate answers. Don't shame him for touching his own genitals, although you can start to teach him about privacy. Tell him that the best place to do this is in his own bedroom or the bathroom. But remember, it is his body and he has the right to touch it. (But you have the right to set the rules about where in the house this is allowed.) It is also a good time to teach him that no one else has the right to touch his body except his doctor. If someone else tries to touch his private parts, he should come and tell you right away.

- Friends become more important in children's lives at this age. Your child needs contact with other kids either through playdates, preschool, or just time with friends on the block. He'll still need help learning "social skills" or simply, how to get along with other people. Make sure to help him resolve conflicts with friends or fights about sharing. Teaching these skills now is an important part of your child getting along with others in the future. If your child's friends act aggressively, explain the house rules ("In this house, we don't hit..."). If that doesn't work, end the playdate and talk to his or her parents about what happened. Don't let your child bully or be bullied. If you see this happening—step in.

- By the age of five, start helping your child to see things from other people's points-of-view. This will help him be more considerate of others' feelings and be a better friend. For example, if she doesn't let a friend join a group game, ask her how she thinks that makes her friend feel.

Continue to help your child become a "decent" person by helping her figure out right from wrong. Being a good role model is the most powerful and effective way to do this.

Discipline for 3 to 5 Year Olds

Your child's language and thinking have grown a lot. When he does something wrong, explain what he did that was wrong and why it's not okay. Help him understand how his behavior might make other people feel. For instance, if he pushes someone when he's frustrated, you might say, "I can see that you're really frustrated. But it's not okay for you to hurt other people when you're angry. You need to use your words to solve problems. When you pushed John, that made him feel sad. You need to say sorry to him." Remember: Praise your child after he makes his apology and tell him that was the right thing to do.

Ignore annoying, but non-dangerous behaviors. By not paying attention to these behaviors, they will disappear over time because they are not rewarded with attention.

BEHAVIORS TO IGNORE:

Whining
Yelling
Pouting
Begging for things in the store
Fussing
Complaining
Unable to play alone (even though
   you've given her lots of one-on-one time already)
Noisiness

BEHAVIORS NOT TO IGNORE:

Hitting
Biting
Kicking
Destroying property on purpose
Scratching
Running into the street
Hurting an animal
Throwing things at people or animals

Praise, praise, praise. Remember to praise positive behaviors as soon as they happen. This teaches your child what to do.

When you discipline your child for something she did wrong, send the message that she's a good girl, but her behavior was not acceptable. It's very important that your child does not get the message that she is a bad person. She is trying to figure out who she is. If she thinks that her mistakes make her a bad person, her self-esteem will suffer.

Because she seems older and more capable, you might find yourself expecting more of her. But remember, she's still quite young. Be realistic. Temper tantrums will still pop up, because she's still not fully in control of her feelings.

FOR AGGRESSIVE ACTS, USE TIME-OUTS. Time-outs work! For some behaviors, you'll need to use time-out. These include anytime your child is aggressive or breaks one of the safety limits you have set (like don't go outside without a grown-up, don't touch the knives). Remember these things:

• Be consistent. Every time she breaks the rule, she must receive a time out. Otherwise she won't know if you really mean it.

• Never threaten time-out. Just give it every time he breaks one of the rules. Threatening doesn't change the behavior.

• Stay calm. Time-outs work. Shouting and yelling don't. Give the time-out as soon as the rule is broken. If you wait too long, she won't learn as quickly from her mistakes.

• Set a timer. Time-outs should equal the age of the child: two minutes for a two-year-old, three minutes for a three-year-old. Never put him in a dark or scary room. Never lock the door.

• If she won't go to time-out, tell her that she will lose a privilege. "You threw a toy at your brother and you are going to time-out. If you don't go to time-out, there will be no TV tonight." Only take away a privilege from that day. For example, don't say there will be no TV or storytime for the week.

• If he messes things up during the time-out, make him clean it up at the end. If he leaves the time-out before it's over, set the timer for one more minute.

• Don't expect to teach her something with one or two time-outs. It might take thirty time-outs before she stops hitting when she's frustrated.

• If you are out shopping, at a restaurant, or anywhere else away from home, take her outside as soon as you can and sit her on a bench. Let her know that the rules are for everywhere!

• Don't hold a grudge. When his time-out is over, greet him with a smile and move on to the next activity.

• While your child is in time-out, no matter what she's done, REMIND YOURSELF OF WHAT A BEAUTIFUL, INCREDIBLE, AMAZING PERSON SHE IS!

If your baby or child is acting up, ask yourself if there's something else going on. Is he tired, hungry, or sick? Is he upset, afraid, or angry about something?

Coping with Tantrums

> I'm trying to get her on the bus, but she wants to go get some candy at the store near the stop. But I tell her "no, we don't have time, here comes the bus." Well, I can see what else is coming besides the bus-a tantrum. Her face starts getting all red. She's falls to the ground and screams "I want candy" real loud. She starts kicking her feet. Now I'm getting steamed. I got this stroller in one hand, I'm trying to pick her up with the other arm. People are looking at me. I wanted to just get on the bus and leave her little screaming behind on the sidewalk.
>
> Latisha, 17 years old

As your baby gets older, he may start acting out his anger and frustration through temper tantrums. Temper tantrums are one of the hardest parts of parenting. Maybe you're having a tough day and on top of that, you have to deal with the meltdowns of your toddler. Even though tantrums are tough to take, almost every child has them and they are a normal part of development. Most temper tantrums happen between the ages of two and three and tend to disappear around the age of five. Basically, a tantrum happens when your child gets more frustrated or angry than he can handle.

A lot of times your child will have a tantrum when she doesn't get her way. Even if it seems like it, she's not trying to drive you crazy. She's not trying to manipulate you or pull one over. It's just normal development. By the age of two, your child is trying to become more independent. She wants to do things her way. When she is denied what she wants, she might have a meltdown. A tantrum is one way they express the confusion and frustration they are feeling. Sometimes, tantrums are her way of trying to control her world. They think by hitting, screaming, or kicking they will get what they want.

Take a minute and think of a few things that trigger your child's tantrums.

My child usually has a tantrum when_____

_____

_____

_____

_____

Another thing that can cause my child to have a tantrum is

_____

_____

_____

_____

Remember to stay calm. Take at least ten deep breaths. Don't let your child's tantrum cause you to have your own tantrum!

Stop Them Before They Start

Tantrums aren't fun for you or your child. Chances are she feels out of control. Unfortunately, you can't eliminate all tantrums. They happen. But you can cut down on the number your child has by following a few steps.

- **Well-rested children** have fewer tantrums. Make sure your child is getting plenty of sleep at night and napping during the day. Tired children are cranky children. If your two-year-old is going to bed at ten o'clock every night, she's likely to be tired and have more meltdowns.

- **Children who feel a lot of stress** in the house have **more tantrums**. Do every thing in your power to keep things calm. If you're living with your mom or dad, ask them to help you with this. Calmer houses make calmer kids!

- **Follow a routine.** Kids are calmer when they know what's coming.

- **Don't say no unless you have to.** Pick your battles! If she wants to wear a pajama top to school, who cares? Ask yourself, "Is it worth a tantrum?" Stopping her from touching a hot stove requires a "no." Wearing two different color shoes probably doesn't. Watching violent television requires a "no." Eating her cereal on the floor like a puppy probably doesn't.

- If you see a tantrum coming, try and **distract** her. Pick her up and look out the window. Start talking. "See the kitty?

What does a kitty say? Wow, look at that truck. What color is that truck?"

Ride it Out

I get so mad at her when she starts in on one of her tantrums. Lately it seems like it's been happenin' a lot. She starts screaming in this loud voice tellin' everyone that she hates me. Then I start screaming at her that she better knock it off. I have a really hard time. I just can't think straight when she does that. Sometimes, I hate to say it, but I just want to smack her and make her stop. What should I do?

Gina, 17 years old

So what should you do in the middle of a tantrum? Excellent question. The first and most important thing is to stay as calm as you can. Melting down or losing control yourself will not help anything. In fact, it will just make your child feel more scared and unsafe than he already does. Take a deep breath and follow the list below.

Tantrum Tips

KEEP COOL. The calmer you are, the faster and easier the whole thing will blow over. Take a few breaths. Remind yourself, tantrums are normal.

Ignore the negative behavior as much as you can. If she learns that tantrums get her what she wants, she'll keep using them. Firmly set a limit and stick with it. If the rule is you can't climb up onto the windowsill (good rule, mom!), then that's that. Keep taking her off the windowsill no matter how hard she screams.

If she's having a full-blown tantrum and distracting her didn't work, put her in a **safe place.** Let her go at it where she won't hurt herself or others.

If he does start physically hurting himself or someone else during a tantrum, you may have to **firmly hold him** to keep him safe. But don't pin him down or put your body on him.

If you're out on the street and your child melts down, get him **out of harm's way**. Don't let him run into the street. Guide him to a quiet place or put him in the stroller until he calms down. Don't let other people staring at you make you feel bad. Everyone has gone through it. Your child's tantrums don't mean you are a bad mother!!! Remember that.

After the tantrum, **don't hold a grudge.** Your child didn't do it to hurt you. She didn't know a better way to express how she felt. Hold her, talk to her, and let it go!

It Won't Last Forever

Your child's tantrums won't last forever. Soon, because you're teaching her how to understand and express her feelings (see Chapter 11), she'll be able to cope with anger and frustration without a tantrum. But for now, it's your job to help her through these explosions safely. Every time you get through a tantrum, pat yourself on the back. And just know that you're one step closer to having them be a distant memory!

When You Don't See Eye-to-Eye

I try really hard to stick with the time-outs because I know for my son they really work. But his father thinks that it's too much trouble. If he misbehaves when he's with him, he either smacks him on the behind or just yells at him to cut it out. Plus, my baby's father doesn't follow a lot of the rules I'm trying to have with our son. I'm trying real hard to show him that manners are important, but his daddy doesn't make him do those things when he's with him. It's just real frustrating. And I can see it confuses my son because there seem to be two sets of rules depending on who he's with.

Jacqueline, 19 years old

In a perfect world, everyone taking care of our children would agree on the same limits and use the same discipline. But in reality, it doesn't usually happen that way. As your child gets older, she will definitely notice these differences and may use them to pressure you to change your rules, "But Dad lets me eat cookies before dinner." "C'mon, Mom says I'm allowed to watch this program." There may be different rules in different houses, but some rules should be the same no matter where your child is, especially rules about safety or health. So what's the best way to get on the same page as the child's other parent? Take a look below for some ideas.

Stay calm and communicate your feelings without attacking the other person. You might start the conversation with a compliment. "You're a great mom/dad and I know you want the best for Jose. I feel like it's really important that he goes to bed by eight o'clock during the week days otherwise he's cranky and tired at school. What do you think?"

Pick your battles. You and your baby's other parent won't agree on everything. No two parents do. Only insist on the things that are most important to the health and safety of the child. When you are unable to resolve issues about the baby, maybe you could decide on a person you both trust to help you.

Concentrate on what you can do. Even if you can't control how your child's other parent disciplines, you do have complete control over what you do. Set reasonable limits, be consistent, and praise lots!

 **STOP AND THINK**

Write down one or two discipline issues that you and your child's other parent don't agree on.

Discipline issues we just don't agree on include

_____
_____
_____
_____
_____
_____

My game plan for dealing with this positively is

_____
_____
_____
_____
_____
_____

My backup plan is

_____
_____
_____
_____
_____
_____

Getting a Schedule Means Getting a Break

Today when my son was going to bed he gave me a hard time because he was so tired. But I was tired too, and I was hoping to get him in bed so I could just chill a little bit before I started my homework and cleaning up the house. We have no real bedtime schedule. I know we need to get him to bed earlier because he's always real tired during the day and won't wake up to go to daycare. On the other hand, I hate fighting him at night when I'm tired too, so most of the time he just stays up 'til he falls asleep on the couch in front of the TV. But tonight I wanted him in bed and out of the living room. It turned out to be terrible. He was holding onto the crib screaming his head off. Finally, after like twenty-five minutes, he fell asleep. I hate it when he fights bedtime like that because it stresses me out.

Lisa, 18 years old

What was your schedule like before you had your child? Were you on a tight schedule? Or did you do things whenever you wanted and came and went as you pleased? No matter what life was like before, babies and children are usually most happy when life is very predictable—that means they know what will happen and when it will happen. That doesn't mean schedules come naturally. They don't. But even if your two-year-old fights bedtime, he still needs one. In fact, he needs to be in bed by seven or eight p.m. every night—for his sake and for yours. Schedules and routines can start when your baby is four to five months old. All children need schedules. Here's what schedules can do for both of you.

- Rested, well-fed babies and children tend to be happier and easier to manage.

- Schedules give you free time so that you can focus on your needs!

- Schedules make children feel safe and less confused. Children on schedules feel like they have more control over their worlds.

- Transitions, like going to school, going to a sitter, and going to bed, are easier when your child has a schedule.

We know it can be hard to have a schedule when you're living in someone else's house, you're in a shelter, or there really isn't enough space for the baby to have his own room. But there are things you can do to make schedules work even in tight living conditions. First, explain to people in the house how important a schedule is. Tell people how cranky the baby gets the next day if he hasn't gotten enough sleep. Ask people to help by keeping the TV, radio, and conversations quiet during bedtime. Be flexible—even if the baby doesn't have his own room, a dark, quiet corner with a crib can be just as good.

What's Sabotaging Your Child's Schedule

I never seem to get to see my son. While I'm at school, he's in daycare. Then I have to go to work and he stays with my mother. By the time I get home it's nine p.m. and I really want to see him because I miss him so much. But then he ends up staying awake until like eleven-thirty and I have to wake him back up at seven a.m. to get him to day-care. The teachers are always saying that he's too tired and needs more sleep, but then I feel guilty for not spending time with him.

Gina, 17 years old

If you are going to school and working, you probably don't have a lot of extra time on your hands. Being stretched thin means you might not get to see your baby as much as you want. Instead of throwing out your baby's sleep schedule, try to find other time during the week to spend time together. Is there time during the weekend when you can be together? Can you work your schedule so that you can put him to bed one night during the week?

We know it's hard if you can't be with your baby as much as you'd like. But the most important thing is that he's getting loving care from the people taking care of him when you're not there. He knows who his parents are and nobody can replace you. He won't forget about you or trade you in. Make the most of the time that you have with your child. Really focus on him. Try not to spend your time together talking on the phone or watching TV. Even a few minutes a day of really connecting to your child keeps the bond strong. Following his schedule (even if that means seeing him less) might be hard for you, but it's good for him!

Finding a Schedule that Works and Sticking with It

Schedules are just habits. You do it for a while and it sticks. If your child's bedtime habit is falling asleep in front of the TV every night, that will become what he expects. But don't worry, schedules can be changed. It won't happen overnight. It'll take a few weeks for him to get used to his new schedule.

People have lots of different beliefs and attitudes about how to get your baby to sleep. Some people are comfortable letting them cry for a while. Some people want to rock their baby to sleep. Some people like to sleep in the same bed as their baby. No matter which way you choose, be aware that you are training your child. If you train him to fall asleep by himself in his crib, he will. If you fall asleep next to him every night, that's what you train him to expect.

Getting Him to Sleep

By the age of six months, you can put your baby in his crib at eight p.m. and expect him to fall asleep on his own. This will take some practice. All learning takes practice. But if you set up this sleep schedule, he'll get used to it. There are some steps you can take to train him more effectively. Think about it. Would you fall asleep if you were out at a club dancing and hanging with your friends? No way. You'd want to stay with the action. So does your baby. You can't expect your baby to be pulled away from the excitement of the house and plunked into bed cold turkey. It won't work!

Try these tips that are proven bedtime winners.

- Do the three B's every night: Bath, Books, and Bed. Bathing your baby and reading to him settle him down and show him that you are on the relaxing and peaceful path to sleep. Calm babies are much more likely to fall asleep. Try not to skip a step. Your baby will notice and will feel kicked off his routine.

- No loud playing and running around after six p.m. Evening is for winding down.

- Keep his room quiet and dim. A nightlight can help give him a sense of safety.

- Put him down in bed and sing a song. Rub his back as you sing. If he starts crying, you keep singing. Leave the room with a cheerful, soft "good night."

- If he cries for more than ten minutes, go in and comfort him with a pat on the back and a calm voice.

- If he cries for ten more minutes do the same thing, but this time don't touch him. Tell him in a calm voice that he'll be okay.

- This may take weeks. But don't give up. If you go in and pick him up, he will cry louder and longer the next time.

Other Sleep Troubles

My three-and-a-half-year-old daughter will not stay in bed. We put her down and about five minutes later she's in the doorway staring at us. If we put her back, she either screams bloody murder or just gets back out. Sometimes I just lose my cool and start yelling at her. But that totally doesn't work. HELP (for real)!

Denise, 20 years old

Maybe you haven't had a solid bedtime schedule before, but realize you and your child need one fast! Or maybe you had one, but your child has suddenly decided she's playing by a new set of rules. Whatever the case, sometimes kids need a little help following the bedtime game plan. This is your chance to try out the parenting secret weapon—the behavior modification plan. **Behavior modification charts** can be used with kids as young as two and a half. It's guaranteed to fix any problem as long as you stick with it faithfully. Here's how it works.

Let's take Shana's problem. Her daughter keeps getting out of bed. So, Shana needs to get a good schedule going and stick with it. She is going to start a star chart (a behavior modification plan). Check it out below:

	Monday	Tuesday	Wednesday	Thursday	Friday	Saturday	Sunday
Tiffany's Stay-in-Bed Chart							
Stay in Bed	★	★	★	★		★	★

A gold star = an extra story the next day.

Six gold stars in one week earns a (any small reward your child may want).

Here's what she will say to Tiffany about one hour before going to bed:

You do so many great things. You help put away your toys. You play nicely with your cousins. And you are a great help with your little sister. But one thing you need to do better at is staying in bed at night. So I'm going to show you what we're going to do to help you get better at this. This is called a star chart. If you stay in your bed at night, the next morning you can get up and put a gold star on your chart. That's pretty cool, huh? And if you stay in bed, then the next day you get an extra story at bedtime.

*If you get out of bed, then you get **no gold star** the next day. And the best part of this is that if you get six gold stars in one week, then you get a special treat. (Have your child make a list of all the things she might want as a reward.) Okay, so now it's bedtime.*

You've had your story. You've gone to the potty. Is there anything else you need? Good. Okay, I love you and I'll see you in the morning.

Leave the room.

If your child stays in bed for the whole night...

- Make a big fuss about it the next day.
- Brag to your mother, boyfriend, or anyone else in the house so that she hears you.
- Let her put her star on the chart.
- Remind her about the extra story she has earned.
- Read the extra story that night and remind her why she's getting an extra story.

If your child is in bed, but screaming for you....

- Make sure she is okay and ignore her.
- Do not yell things back to her or start a discussion.
- Remember she's trying to get your attention. Don't give her any.

If your child gets out of bed...

- Tell her she has lost her story for the next day and she gets no star.
- Calmly put her right back to bed
- Do not argue, fight, pull her, or yell. Let the chart do the work.

- If she gets out again, put her right back.

- Do this as many times as she gets out of bed.

This will take some time—up to two weeks (or even more). Don't give up. **Letting her stay up just once will undo all the work you've done.**

Star Charts Can Change Almost Any Behavior

Behavior modification plans can change almost any problem behavior if you follow the program! We won't kid you—behavior modification programs can be a lot of work on your end, but they are very, very effective and will save you a lot of grief in the long run. Sure, it takes some effort to train your child to go to sleep, but think what you gain—hours and hours of peace. Here's how to set up a simple behavior modification plan.

First thing you need to do is figure out the behaviors that you want to change. Is it whining, fighting, not picking up toys?

Identify the opposite behavior. This is called the **"positive opposite."** Look at the positive opposite for the behaviors above:

Problem Behavior	**Positive Opposite**
Whining	Speaking in a normal voice
Refusing to take a bath	Bathing
Fighting at toothbrushing time	Brushing teeth cooperatively
Not picking up toys	Picking up toys
Fighting with peers	Playing nicely with peers

(Kazdin, 2005)

• Put two or three of the positive opposite behaviors on the chart. We'll call them **target behaviors**. Don't try to change too many things at once. Go slowly.

• **Reward every time!** Every single time your child does one of the positive or target behaviors, put a star on the chart and praise him. This means that you have to pay attention to what your child is doing. For example, if he is aggressive and you are trying to get him to play cooperatively with his friends, then **you have to watch him play so that you can catch him playing nicely.** If he shares, helps a friend, deals with frustration positively, you must catch this and reward it. DOING THIS WILL CHANGE HIS BEHAVIOR.

• If your child reaches the number of points he needed to get his reward, give him the reward that day, no matter how bad his behavior may have been. This is very important. It won't work if you don't follow this step!

Example #1 Star Chart for a Two-Year-Old

James's Star Chart							
	Monday	Tuesday	Wednesday	Thursday	Friday	Saturday	Sunday
Stand still for Mom or Dad to brush teeth	★	★	★	★		★	★
Take off clothes for bathtime	★		★			★	
Put on pajamas	★	★				★	
Put away toys before bed		★	★			★	

Fifteen gold stars in one week earns a *(any small reward your child may want)*.

Example #2 Star Chart for a Five-Year Old

Jenny's Star Chart							
	Monday	Tuesday	Wednesday	Thursday	Friday	Saturday	Sunday
No tantrums when Mom says "No"	★ ★	★ ★	★ ★	★ ★	★ ★	★ ★ ★	★
Talk or play nicely with sister	★ ★ ★	★ ★	★		★ ★ ★	★ ★	★ ★
No whining or begging in stores	★	★ ★	★			★ ★	★

Thirty gold stars in one week earns a *(any small reward your child may want)*.

A Few Tips on Behavior Charts

How Many Stars Does She Need to Get a Treat?

To start, choose a number of stars that she can reasonably earn. Too high and she'll get discouraged. Too low and she won't try very hard. Don't expect her to change her behavior overnight. You are teaching her something new, and it will take time. For example, if you want her to pick up her toys every night, but right now she never does it when you ask her to, start off with her having to do it three nights a week to get the reward. Then slowly increase the number of stars she needs to earn the reward.

Change the Reward

Sometimes kids will get bored with a certain reward. So you'll have to mix it up to keep them interested. It doesn't have to break the bank. It just needs to be something he'll work for.

Be Specific

Only put behaviors on the chart that you can see with your own eyes. A young woman in one of our groups wrote on her five-year-old son's behavior chart, "Be Good." But the problem was, nobody knew exactly what that meant. So we helped her get more specific. Every time her son did what she asked him to do with no fight (like wash your hands for dinner), he got a sticker on his chart. Every time he played with his brother for thirty minutes without hitting him, he got a sticker. Every time he said "please" or "thank you," he got a sticker.

Star Chart Exercise: Write down your most challenging discipline situation that occurs with your child. Now, create a behavior modification chart to help change this behavior. Use the chart on the next page to help you. Remember to:

• Choose specific target behaviors you can see with your eyes!

• Find the positive opposite of the problem behavior.

• Reward the behavior every time it happens.

• Choose a reasonable number of times the child must do the behavior to get the reward.

• Always give positive praise along with the star or sticker on the chart.

• Brainstorm with the child what reward she wants to work for.

Star Chart

	Monday	Tuesday	Wednesday	Thursday	Friday	Saturday	Sunday
Write good behavior in box							

_____ stars/checks/points in one week earns a *(any small reward your child may want)*.

Children Need Love to Grow Strong

What's the real point of discipline? To raise healthy, happy, and kind people who know right from wrong and make good choices in life. The fact is, kids who feel really loved are more likely to be good listeners. That doesn't mean that your well-loved child will always act the way you want, but it does mean that he or she will probably have fewer behavior problems than kids who don't feel loved. So really, discipline starts with parents showing lots of love. To help your child feel loved, do these simple things every day.

• Tell your child you love him.

• Hug your child a lot.

• Let your child know you are proud of her

for who she is.

Chapter 13

Breaking the Cycle

I got pregnant when I was sixteen years old. I guess you could say I had a pretty messed-up life before that. From my earliest memories my mother was on drugs. My father walked out on us when I was two. I had five brothers and sisters and we were put in foster care and didn't get to see each other. I went to four different foster homes, and at two of them I was sexually abused. When I was fifteen I ran away from my last placement and started living with a guy who was seven years older than me. I thought I finally found someone to take care of me, but I was wrong. It wasn't a good relationship because he was always running around on me, lying, and leaving me at home alone with the baby. I was scared and I really didn't have anyone to help me. I had no idea how to take care of a baby.

I guess you could say I'm one of the lucky ones, though. I found out from people in my old neighborhood where one of my older sisters was living and went to her apartment one day. It turns out she had a child and I learned a lot from being with her. Somehow she had figured out how to give her baby all the things we missed out on from our mother, like love, patience, and attention. Plus my sister helped me out with babysitting so that I could find a job. I worked mad hard going to school during the day and working at a grocery store at night. It wasn't easy. Sometimes I didn't think I could make it, but my sister and her boyfriend helped me and I kept going.

When my little girl was three, I had my GED and finished a computer training program. Soon I got a job as a secretary where I got health insurance. Now I'm making enough to support me and my daughter, and that makes me feel really proud considering that I did it all on my own. We have our own apartment finally. I guess you could say I'm standing on my own two feet now. Don't get me wrong—it's still hard. I don't really have time to date or hang out that much, but it's cool. I feel like I can take care of us, and that's what counts.

Looking back, I was way too young to have a kid, but I can't imagine my life without her. Having her has made me strong. I'm a better person because of her.

Denise, 20 years old

Our Own Childhoods

What does the word "childhood" mean to you? When you think of your own younger childhood, what memories, images, and feelings come up? Take a few minutes and think back as far as you can. What are your very first memories of being alive? Was your house filled with warmth and joy? What do you remember feeling as a very young child? For some people their early childhoods are packed with memories of happiness, love, and support. But for others, we carry memories of fear, sadness, anxiety, or worry. And others think back to when they were very young and find both kinds of memories—good and painful. Believe it or not, the kind of childhood you had is a powerful factor in determining the kind of childhood your child has. But let's be clear—the past doesn't have to predict the future. What we mean is that even if your early childhood was unhappy, you have the power to create a warm, happy, secure life for your child. But that requires you to look at some of the ghosts in your past and let them go.

So what are ghosts of the past? Well, by ghosts of the past we mean the unhappy experiences that occurred in your life that sometimes come up again and again until you make a choice to face them and start healing them.

Seeing Ghosts

A lot of times the ghosts of our pasts are things that happen in families over and over again. They become cycles of family problems and include:

- **Drug and Alcohol Addiction**

- **Prison**

- **Physical, Emotional, and Sexual Abuse**

- **Not Knowing a Parent**

- **Domestic or Relationship Abuse**

- **Teenage Pregnancy**

- **Neglect**

- **Putting Men (or Women) Before the Needs of a Child**

Each of these ghosts is a very important issue and we could write a whole book about every one of them. But we are not going to spend a lot of time talking about each one simply because we don't have the space. We wrote another book called **Power Source: Taking Charge of Your Life** which deals with all the family problems listed above. You can get this book by asking your counselor, teacher, or a librarian to contact the Lionheart Foundation.

But there are a few things we would like to say about healing the ghosts of your past while raising a baby.

It's never too late. Even if you have spent a lot of time running away from these problems because they are too difficult to face, every moment of every day is a new chance to look at the pain you may have experienced and start to deal with it. Making this choice not only frees you from the pain of the past, but means that you are choosing not to pass it on to your baby. This doesn't mean that healing is always easy. A lot of the time it can bring up painful and difficult feelings. In the long run, however, it gives you more control over your life.

Family problems tend to get passed down unless you actively choose to stop them. Like we talked about in the discipline section, we learn what we see. If you watched people handle stress by drinking or using drugs, this may be the way that you self-soothe or cope with the world. If your baby watches you do any of these things, chances are he'll learn the same from you. All of the ghosts we listed above are family cycles. You can make the choice to stop the cycle. But ignoring the problem won't make it disappear.

Drugs and Alcohol

I started drinking when I was 12 'cuz I was hanging out with an older crowd. Real fast it turned into smoking weed, but the alcohol was what really messed me up bad. Pretty soon I was drinking every day, sometimes before school. I'm ashamed of it now, but I was even drinking when I was pregnant with Riah. I knew I shouldn't because the doctors told me how it could hurt her, but even those warnings didn't make me change. When she was born, I was way stressed out. She cried all the time and I was drinking more and more to try and chill out and handle the stress. Those were the worst days of my life 'cuz you can't take care of yourself or a baby when you're drunk or passed out on the couch like I was. Even when I wasn't drunk, I wasn't really there for Riah 'cuz I was always thinking about when I could get a drink. My aunt is a recovering alcoholic and she got all up in my face about it. At first I was pissed off like she had no right tellin' me what to do. Then she threatened to call OSS if I didn't get help. I thank God for that now, but when I was drinkin' I just couldn't see the truth.

I thought I controlled the drinkin', but really it controlled me. Worse than that, for a long time it messed up me being a good mother to my daughter.

Louisa, 19 years old

Sometimes we make the mistake of thinking that drugs and alcohol will fix our problems. We trick ourselves into believing that drinking will take away the pain of hurtful childhoods or that getting high will help us escape difficult feelings like stress, anger, and sadness. And for a short time, drugs and alcohol might numb you so you forget what's really upsetting you or change your mood. But the deeper truth is that **abusing substances doesn't solve anything.** Ever. When we sober up or come down, our problems are still there, only they're usually much worse. Plus, we feel like we've let down ourselves, our children, and the people around us.

STOP AND THINK

If you grew up in a house where one or more of your caregivers was using, ask yourself how that felt. Were they able to show up for you as responsible parents? Or did the alcohol and drugs prevent them from giving you the attention, safety, love, and support you needed? Did you grow up feeling cheated because of your parents' addictions? Did you have to "act like the parent" sometimes? Did it leave you feeling ashamed of your family or yourself? This is what most kids experience when they grow up in substance abusing families.

Now ask yourself: ***Is this what I want for my child?***

Parenting Under the influence

We all know that substance use is never a healthy choice, **but the stakes are even higher when you're a parent.** Using substances when you're pregnant or parenting is like playing with a loaded gun. Now you aren't just putting your own health on the line, you're risking your baby's safety. And that's no joke.

Risks to *Your Baby* When You Use

- If you are pregnant and drinking or using drugs, you're putting your baby at risk each time you tip the bottle, light up, snort, sniff, or inject. Babies exposed to drugs and alcohol can develop life-threatening health issues and developmental problems. **The sooner you stop, the healthier your baby will be.**

- If you are drinking or using substances, you are not able to supervise your baby or child as well as if you were sober. **Unsupervised children are much more likely to get hurt.**

- Children who grow up with substance or alcohol abusing parents **do worse in school, have more emotional problems, and have a harder time socially.**

- If you drink or use in front of your child, **you are teaching him or her to use.**

- **Be Real.** If you are using, drugs and alcohol are robbing your baby of the time, patience, and money she deserves. Parents who are drunk or high cannot be there emotionally for their children, giving them the love they need.

Risks to *You* When You Use

• You're more likely to get a sexually transmitted disease or pregnant when you are drunk or high because you're less likely to use protection.

• You're more likely to engage in other high-risk behaviors like fighting, stealing or driving too fast because your judgment is worse and your inhibitions (the part of your mind that tells you *not* to get involved in risky behavior) are lowered.

• Certain substances are addictive and make you become **physically dependent** on them. All drugs and alcohol can do serious damage to your body over time.

• Drug and alcohol use can prevent you from developing healthy ways to cope with your problems. This makes you become **psychologically dependent** on them as a way to deal with the world.

• It is **impossible** to have mature, stable, honest relationships when you (or your partner) is using.

• Using keeps you from getting ahead in life. It's almost impossible to keep a job or do well in school.

• You cannot be a safe or effective parent when you're using drugs or alcohol. And you're more likely to lose custody of your child if you have a substance abuse problem you don't get help for.

Taking Control

The first step to taking control over your substance use to admit there is a problem. Like Louisa said, denial keeps us from coming clean. But until you admit you have a problem, you can't deal with it. If you know you've got a substance use problem but haven't found the strength to get help, **do it for your child. And do it now.** Ask yourself if this is what you want to pass down to him-- the legacy of a lost childhood and a cycle of addiction. Because this is exactly how it happens. Not year by year, but day by day. **Each moment you are using is a moment he is losing.**

There are people who can help you get a handle on your drug or alcohol problem. You aren't alone and you aren't the only one facing this fight. Thousands of young parents struggle with addiction. The sooner you reach out for help, the safer you and your baby will be. If you can't find a program in your community, call one of these hotline numbers. They'll help you get in touch with people to get you on the road to recovery and one step closer to regaining your power and being the kind of parent you can be proud of.

National Youth Crisis Hotline
1-800-448-4663
1-800-422-0009

Alcohol and Drug Helpline
1-800-527-5344
www.aca-usa.org

Substance Abuse Treatment Facility Locator
1-800-662-HELP
www.findtreatment.samhsa.gov

The truth is:

You are stronger than any addiction.
You are deeper than any urge.
You are larger than any problem in your life.
And your baby deserves a parent who is totally there for him.

The Ghost of Teenage Pregnancy

It's so strange how all of these coincidences keep happening. My baby's father and I split up when my daughter was two months old. I was sitting in a restaurant with my dad when I told him and he started crying because I was the exact same age when he and my mom split up. Another thing is that me and my mom got pregnant for the first time at the same age. We were both seventeen. I'm not saying that if your mom got pregnant young, you have to do the same thing. But it does seem that it happens that way a lot.

Lacy, 21 years old

STOP AND THINK

So far in this book we haven't talked a lot about why people get pregnant at a very young age. Before looking at the reasons other people have given as to why they got pregnant really young, ask yourself what was going on for you. Be kind to yourself as you ask this question, but honest. Maybe you never even thought of getting pregnant as a choice you made. Maybe it seemed like it just happened. Even if you can't come up with a reason as to why you got pregnant, think about some of the things that were happening in your life that led you to getting pregnant. Understanding why we make the choices we do gives us greater power and control over our lives. Don't think about what other people said about your pregnancy—look in your heart and ask yourself why you think you became a young parent. If you would like to write any of these reasons down, take a moment to do it.

We asked some young women in a group why they think they got pregnant and become a parent at a young age and here's what they said:

I think I was looking to have someone to always love me. I never got that from my own family, so I thought having a baby would give me that—a person to love me and someone I could love back.

Christine, 17 years old

For me, having a baby was a way to prove to everyone that I wasn't a little kid. I'd been taking care of myself my whole life. I thought having a baby would get me the respect I thought I deserved.

Shana, 16 years old

My mom was never really there for me unless something really bad happened. Like once I got arrested and she showed up at the police station at two in the morning. Part of me thinks I got pregnant so she would be part of my life the way I always wanted her to be by helping me raise the baby.

Erica, 19 years old

Honestly, I had this fantasy in my head of having the perfect family like I would see in the movies or on TV. Everyone always says that it's not for real, but that's what I wanted deep in my heart. I wanted to make a family with a mother who took care of the kids and a father who went to work and looked after his family. I thought if I got pregnant that my boyfriend wouldn't leave me because for the rest of our lives we'd have this bond. The baby. But it didn't turn out that way. He promised he'd never leave me, but about three months after the baby was born, he was outta here.

Allysa, 15 years old

Nothing I did seemed to work out. I wasn't good at school. Didn't feel so good about my future. Didn't really feel like I could get a decent job. But I knew I could be a mother. That was something I felt like I could be for sure.

Monique, 16 years old

That's what everybody in my family did, have a baby real young. Plus all my friends were having them, so I was like, why not? I didn't want to be left out.

Carrie, 17 years old

I wanted to change my life because it was so bad. I didn't know exactly what it would be like to have a baby, but it couldn't be any worse than what my life was like. I thought having a baby might make things different or better for me.

Gina, 17 years old

I was so used to taking care of everyone in my family, like my four sisters and brothers, because my mother is an addict and was never around. I thought this is what God had in store for me, to take care of everyone. I started being a mother to my siblings when I was twelve, so why not be a mother to my own child when I was sixteen?

Maia, 17 years old

I thought having a baby would give me something to feel proud of. Something that people would say, "Oh what a cute baby that is." All my life I felt like people looked down on me like I was nobody. But having a sweet, pretty baby would be a way to have something to feel proud of.

Shaniqwa, 19 years old

I was doing real good at school before I got pregnant. My teachers were always keeping brochures for me that came from colleges. They thought I was smart and could really go somewhere. Deep down, I think I had a baby so that I couldn't go to college. I was afraid I wouldn't make it there. Afraid of being out in the world on my own. Now I'm living with my mom, raising the baby. Sometimes I wonder what it would have been like if I didn't have the baby and went to college. I'm still going to try and go someday, I hope.

Carla, 20 years old

No matter why you got pregnant, you have the power to become an effective and amazing parent right now! But taking a hard, honest look at the reasons for becoming a parent as a very young person means that you might help your child from doing the same thing. Understanding our own behavior is the first step in breaking cycles we want to stop. It also means you will have more control over if and when you have another child in the future. We aren't judging you or saying that you aren't a great parent (if you are reading this book, we're sure you are!). **Being a very young parent is not wrong, but it is hard.** It's a big challenge to raise a child when you're still growing so much yourself. One of the things that really wise and effective parents do is take every step they can to help their child have an easier, more secure life than they did.

STOP AND THINK

Write a letter to your own young child or baby giving him or her advice about becoming a young parent. Imagine you have your child's full attention. What wisdom would you like to pass on? What would you like him or her to know before making the choice to become a parent?

Mistakes of the Past

I'm scared of what the future will bring me. I feel scared that my daughter will notice a lot of my mistakes from when I was younger and that she will throw it in my face. For example, like when I got pregnant at the age of fourteen. I'm scared that my daughter around that age will be like "Hey Mom, I'm pregnant, but you can't say anything about it." I feel like I will be left with nothing to say. Or like me and her father have a lot of tattoos. I feel like one is okay, but I don't want her to have as many as I have. Maybe I'll tell her that if she *finishes college she can have as many as she wants. And when she's finished, she'll be smart enough to get none! But seriously, I want to do something with my life so she doesn't look at me and just think I made mistakes, but that I really did something with my life. Maybe she'll be inspired to make something of herself, too.*

Gina, 17 years old

Because family problems tend to get passed down, you might have already been in a pattern of high-risk behavior before you became a parent. Or maybe your family hasn't seen a lot of the ghosts we talked about before, but you had made some choices that you wished you hadn't. As parents, many of us worry about the mistakes we made and wonder if our children will be hurt by them. But the truth is that children are affected much more by what you are doing now—from day to day—than they are by what you did two, three, four, or five years ago. If you show up for your child as a responsible, caring, decent, loving parent, it doesn't matter how many tattoos you have or how old you were when you got pregnant. Working on yourself and healing the ghosts of the past (by going to counseling, finding a mentor, reading books like this one, attending parenting classes, and spending time with your baby) are the best ways to keep your child from making the same mistakes that you did!

Making Mistakes Now

I'm not making excuses for what I did. It was flat-

out wrong. But that day I was really stressed out. The baby's father was supposed to pick him up and he was late again. So I was late for work and my boss told me that one more time showing up late meant that I was fired. Plus, I didn't have the rent money this month on account of I had to spend it on the car so I could get to my job. Anyways, my son was acting up and hit his cousin so that both of the kids were screaming and crying. Then he turned around and hit me. I just lost it and smacked him across the face. Right after I did it, I felt so horrible. I took some deep breaths until I got myself under control. Then I apologized to him and said that Mommy was wrong to hit him and I was sorry for what I did.

Denise, 20 years old

Not all of our mistakes are in the past. Being a parent is hard work and most of us mess up every day. Some mistakes are small, like dropping her off at daycare and forgetting the diaper bag. Some mistakes are big, like when we hurt our child by accident or because we lost control. Even though making mistakes comes with the territory, it's important that we take responsibility for our errors and try to make them right. Here are a few tips that can help.

Dealing with Mistakes

1. Congratulate yourself for realizing you made a mistake. Knowing that you made a mistake is the first step to making things right. Plus, realizing you've made a mistake makes it harder for family problems like physical abuse to become patterns. Seeing the problem is the first step in stopping the cycle.

2. Take full responsibility for your mistake. This step can be hard, but it's important. If you hit your child, but blame it on the child for making you angry, this is not accepting responsibility. This is called rationalizing your behavior, and it keeps family problems going. If you did something unfair or impulsive, like break one of his toys because he ruined something of yours, you must make it right. Only by showing our children decent and respectful behavior can we expect them to act this way themselves.

3. Apologize and talk it through. Offering your child a genuine apology is a powerful way to begin healing both big and little mistakes. Also, take the time to talk through with your child why you made the mistake. For example, if you do hit your child, you might say: "I am very sorry that I hit you. Mommy is very tired and I lost my temper. What I did was wrong and I am very sorry." Make sure your apology doesn't include blaming the child. No matter how angry our children make us, they don't deserve to get hit.

4. Make it right. Saying sorry for hurting your child or making a mistake is important, but it's not enough. We also have to try and fix the harm we've done. If you lost your child's favorite toy, replace it. If you've hit him, take the time to soothe him. Ask what you can do to make him feel better. It might be playing a game, reading a book, or anything else that shows him you are working to fix the harm you caused. Trying to make things better is also a very important step in teaching him how to fully take responsibility for his wrong actions.

5. Make a plan for the next time. We all lose our cool or make choices we regret as parents. Having a plan in place for the next time can be a great way to prevent these mistakes from happening again. For example, if you have hit your child several times when you feel stressed out, get a plan ready for the next time it happens. Leave the room, breathe fifteen times deeply, or do anything else that will keep you from hurting your child. Practice the plan several times before you actually need it.

6. Forgive yourself. After you have taken responsibility for your mistake and apologized, forgive yourself. Do your best to let it go. Hanging on to guilt or beating yourself up over and over doesn't solve anything. Parenting is a hard job and nobody does it perfectly. Forgiving yourself doesn't mean that what you did was okay. If you hurt your child, it is very important you take full responsibility. Forgiving yourself means that you give yourself another chance to be the best parent you can. Forgiveness means you see your Core Self, the always good, kind, and decent person trying hard to do the right thing. Forgiving means that you pick yourself up after a mistake and move on with an open and loving heart.

If Your Child Gets Taken Away

I can't say it wasn't my fault that I lost custody of Taisha. I wasn't taking care of her like I should have been. Sometimes I would leave her with my little sister so I could go out and party with my friends. Then one time I went out and my sister went over to our cousins' house for what was supposed to be a minute. Turns out she lost track of time and Taisha got left alone in the apartment for something like two hours. She must have been crying for a long time because one of the neighbors finally called the cops. That night when I came back the cops were still there and I walked in high. DSS took her and put her in foster care. It was stupid. I wish I could go back and change things, but I can't. All I can do is stay straight and make all my visitations with her to prove I'm responsible enough to get her back. Sometimes I feel sorry for myself, but it's Taisha who had to pay the price for my actions. At night when I'm going to sleep, I cry and wonder how she is and how her day was.

Lauren, 17 years old

One of the most difficult things that can happen to any parent is having your baby taken away. Losing custody of your child can happen for many different reasons, but the feelings that follow are often the same: shame, fear, anger at the people who took the baby, anger at the people who may have reported you, regret about some of the choices you made, worry about your baby, loss of control, and confusion about what will happen next. Some people who have been struggling with raising a baby under very difficult circumstances might even feel relief that some of the pressure of caring for the baby is off them for a while, but then feel guilt for feeling relieved. All of these are normal reactions. There is no right way to feel when something like this happens.

What Your Child Might Be Feeling

How old your child is when she or he is removed from your care plays a big part in how they feel about being placed in foster care. Very young babies may not have as hard a time as toddlers because they haven't had as long to grow attached to you. Young babies will usually do fine as long as they are fed, soothed, held, and cared for.

Toddlers and older children are more aware of what's going on, so the separation might be more difficult for them. Most likely they are feeling some of the same things you are: scared, alone, uncomfortable living with people they don't know, confused about what's happening, worried that they won't be with you again, angry at you and the people who took them away from you, like the world isn't fair, and sad. Older children sometimes even blame themselves for being taken away. They think that if they had been a better kid and not made so much trouble, they wouldn't have been removed from your care.

Some children might even seem really happy in foster care, especially if they are placed with relatives or a safe, loving family. This is also normal. It doesn't mean your child doesn't miss you or love you anymore. It just means they are doing well and are getting what they need. Instead of feeling rejected, see it as a wonderful gift that your baby is in good hands.

Being Strong Enough to Take the Blame

Experts know that babies and children do better when parents stand up and take responsibility for their child being put in foster care. Why? Because your child needs to know that being placed in foster care is NEVER a child's fault. We know it's hard, but you must take complete responsibility for your child being taken away. Here are some things you might say:

> Mom/Dad made some bad choices. I wish I hadn't, but I did. Now it's up to me to make better choices and prove that I am responsible enough to have you back home with me again. While you're away, I'm learning how to be a better parent so that when you come back, things will be different.

> I just want you to know that nothing you did caused this to happen. This was Mommy/Daddy's fault. I am sorry that you have to go through this. But I want you to know how much I love you and how hard I'll work to get you back.

Getting Your Baby Back

Getting your baby back means showing up as a responsible and involved parent. It means proving that you are ready and able to care for your child better than before. It means growing up and maturing for your sake and his. YOU CAN DO THIS. People who have your best interests at heart want you to be reunited with your child because EVERBODY WINS. Here is a list of things that can help you regain custody of your child and start a positive future together.

Believe in yourself. Know that you have what it takes to be a strong, responsible parent.

Accept that once your baby gets removed from your care, you will have to prove that you are ready to become a parent again.

Let people help you. It's hard to be a parent alone. Go to parenting classes, and let social workers, nurses, and family workers guide you in being the best parent you can be.

Get treatment if you have a drug or alcohol problem. Abusing substances is unsafe for you and your child. Parents who are drunk or high do not make safe choices and place their baby in danger.

Show up for every court date and visitation with your child (if you are allowed to have them). This is evidence that you are responsible and able to care for your child. Listen to the judge or your social worker. If she tells you to go to a parenting class, go. If she tells you not to call or visit your baby, don't.

Get organized. Writing appointments and phone numbers in a safe place is a good way to stay on track with your **reunification plan** (getting your child back).

Use the time your baby is out of your care to improve your life in anyway you can. Use the extra time to finish your GED or study more, get a job, or find a better living situation.

Remember, when you visit toddlers or older children, they might act angry or ignore you. It doesn't mean they don't love you or want to see you. They are protecting themselves from the feelings they have about being separated from you. *No matter what*, you must show them unconditional love, no matter how long they shut you out or are angry. Their reaction is normal and the only way many kids know how to deal with the overwhelming feelings that come with being taken away from their parents.

Let your child know that it's okay to ask questions about what happened. Encourage him to express his feelings about the experience even if they cause you pain. You might not have all the answers, but he will feel safe knowing that he is listened to and that his feelings are respected.

It's normal for a child to melt down, cry, and lose control when a visit with you is over. Although this is hard to watch, it's an honest expression of how he's feeling. Kids are resilient, however. Chances are he'll be playing and laughing in a short time. It's really important for you to reassure him or her that you'll be back and that you love him.

Breathe deeply. Even after you are reunified with your child (living together) he might continue to feel hurt, fear, and anger. Be patient with him and with yourself. The more you can allow him to have his feelings, the more sense he can make out of what happened. Be patient.

Read the section that came before this on **Dealing with Mistakes.**

The biggest reason we need to take responsibility for our mistakes as they happen is so they don't become the ghosts of our children's future. This takes a lot of effort and determination on our part. But it is a gift that will last for generations.

Show Your Love

How many people grew up without ever hearing your parents say, "I love you"? Did you know that not being shown love is also a family problem? And it's a problem you can end by giving your child lots of affection, spending time listening to his thoughts and feelings, and telling him how special he is. You can think of it as nutrition for his heart and soul. And it can help him grow into a healthier, happier person. So remember to do these simple, but powerful things every day.

• Tell your child you love him.

• Hug your child a lot.

• Let your child know you are proud of her for who she is.

Chapter 14

The Future

Sometimes I feel scared of the future. Like what will happen to me and the baby? Will my boyfriend stick with us? I wonder how I'm gonna finish school and what kind of job I'll get. How will I support us both if I'm on my own? Then I just take a deep breath and remind myself to take it one day at a time. As long as I stay on track and do what I need to be doing, I know in my heart it'll work out. I got faith in that. Mostly I'm hopeful about the future. I feel like I'm raising my child the best way I can and that the future is going to be bright for both of us.

Janet, 18 years old

One thing I know is I don't want no drama in my future. My baby isn't gonna be around violence like I was, growing up in the streets. Now that I'm a father, I don't want to always be looking over my shoulder. That's the kind of life I'm leaving behind. What I want is a solid, decent life, like going to work every day, relaxing with my family, and taking care of my business. I always thought that the action of the street was what made life worth living. I wanted the excitement and the rush that went along with the negative acts I was caught up in. But now I see that the only thing in that future is jail or death. I see my homies leaving babies with no fathers to show them right or wrong. If they was still here, I would ask them, "Was it worth it?"

James, 19 years old

What's in Your Future?

Take a minute and write down a vision of what you want your future to look like. What kind of career do you see? What kind of lifestyle? Where would you like to be living? Do you see college in your future? What's in your baby's future? Are friends and family a big part of your life? Include as much detail about this picture as you can. Allow yourself to picture the kind of life you *really* want to build.

My Future:

_____

_____

_____

_____

_____

_____

_____

Getting There

There's nothing harder than being a young parent. Nothing. But the good news is that you have what it takes to get the job done. You already possess the strength, wisdom, and love it takes to be a great parent and create a positive future. One study actually found that being a young mother made people stronger and more focused on their goals! If you're wondering what the future holds for you, you don't need a crystal ball. Look into the mirror, because the future is 100% up to you. If you use the baby as a reason to check out, things will probably stay the same. But if you face your fears and worries with the courage that's already there at the core of who you are, **nothing can stop you.**

Right after I had the baby, I was like, forget it. I can't take care of this baby and go to school and work. I just kind of pulled into a shell and didn't deal with the outside world for a long time. I felt overwhelmed. Plus, part of me felt like having the baby gave me a good reason not to have to accomplish certain things, like graduating from high school or working. I told myself, "I don't have to do those things now that I have a baby to take care of." But part of me knew that unless I finished school and found a job, my life was going nowhere. I'd just be stuck on that couch with no education and no job skills. Stuck in a dead-end life just like my mother was. It was hard to push myself out there, especially in the beginning. But I did. There were days that it felt like it was all crashing down around me and I was like, "What's the point?" But I kept trying and pushed through. Now I got my GED and I'm training to be a medical technician. I'm almost there and I got to say, I'm proud of myself. My grandmother really supported me. When I was about to give up she would say, "If it's worth having, it's worth working for." She was right.

Carla, 20 years old

Getting There Goals

In order to get where we want to go, we have to plan. Having goals is one of the best ways to make your vision about your future a reality. Take a few deep breaths and break it down step by step. Just like building a future, you don't have to finish this exercise in one day. Take your time. Once it's completed, keep it in sight to help you stay focused on what you want and how to get it!

My Child (include goals for your relationship, educational goals, the types of experiences you want to expose him to, helping him develop important skills, and keeping the other parent involved)

Goals for Now:

Goals for Next Year:

Five-year Goals:

My Education (include improving your study skills, passing certain classes, finishing high school, going to college or trade school)

Goals for Now:

Goals for Next Year:

Five-year Goals:

Living Arrangements (include making changes in your current living arrangements to make your parenting more effective, planning for an apartment of your own, selecting the town or neighborhood you want to be in)

Goals for Now:

Goals for Next Year:

Five-year Goals:

Career (include what you want to be "in the future," the skills or training you need to get this job, stepping-stone jobs that will give you the experience you need to land the job you want, characteristics or traits you need to develop to succeed at your job)

Goals for Now:

Goals for Next Year:

Five-year Goals:

Self-Development (include qualities you would like to develop—patience, assertiveness, trust, communication skills. Also include new hobbies you'd like to try or interests you'd like to pursue)

Goals for Now:

Goals for Next Year:

Five-year Goals:

Friendships and Family (include what you will look for in new friendships, how you can be a better friend to the people already in your life, ways you'd like your relationship with family members to change or grow, and the kind of relationships you need to leave behind)

Goals for Now:

Goals for Next Year:

Five-year Goals:

Another Baby?

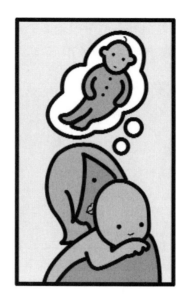

Read my lips! There's no way I'm having another baby until my life changes up big-time. I feel like I can barely handle what's on my plate, so how am I gonna take care of another baby? I would like to have another child in the future. But that time isn't now. I want to feel settled and really be standing on my own two feet. I want to be with a man who's going to really be there for his kids. It's alright. I got time.

Lisa, 18 years old

Before I end up having another baby, I know there's lots of things I have to accomplish first, like driving school and to have my own car because getting around with one baby is hard and it will get even worse with two. I have to be at least eighteen and have my GEO because I want to be a good role model for my kids. I have to be in a bigger apartment and have a stable job as either a hairstylist or a medical assistant. Don't get me wrong, I would love my daughter to have someone to play with and not be so alone. And I don't want my kids to be real far apart in age. But I got to get my life straight before I can really do it right.

Renata, 16 years old

Even though we all know being a young parent is hard work, you might be surprised to know that many young women have another baby soon after the first. They do it for a lot of reasons. Some feel like having another baby will change their situation for the better (it almost never does). They think that having a big family will give them the love that they crave. Or they're with a new guy and want to prove their commitment to him. And honestly, being pregnant and getting a new baby is exciting. But it's a thrill you don't want to get addicted to. Because we all know by now babies are a lot of work! Whatever the reason you might feel like you want another child, be clear on the math: **One baby is a lot of work. Two babies is ten times more.**

 **STOP AND THINK**

In life, the more honest we are with ourselves, the better we can plan and succeed. The only person who can really decide whether you are going to have another child is you! If you aren't standing there saying, "No way do I want another child right now," do this exercise. Write down all of the reasons you might want another child. Then take a minute and ask yourself what the consequences or challenges might be if you do.

Having Another Baby

My real reasons for wanting another child in the near future:

_____

_____

_____

_____

_____

_____

_____

_____

_____

_____

_____

The real consequences if I do (think of how this will
affect the baby you already have):

_____

_____

_____

_____

_____

What has to happen in my life before I'm ready for the next baby
(think of things you have control over):

_____

_____

_____

_____

_____

It's Under Control

We ran a group with twelve young moms a while back. When we asked them if they thought that having another baby was under their control, only two people raised their hand! Only two people! The others said things like, "Well, you know, things happen." Or, "I don't know what the future will bring me." But the truth is, **you do have a lot of control over your future!** Maybe as a kid, things just happened to you, but as a young adult, you get to make the choices about who you're in relationships with,, the kind of work you do, and how you raise your child. Your future is in your hands!

What I Can Control Exercise:

Look at the following list. Write each of these things under the column **Can Control** or **Can't Control.** After you've finished, see which one has more items under it. Take a minute and ask yourself how important it is to be in charge of your life. Do you know anyone who has really taken control over his or her life? What does she do? What kinds of choices has she made? Name three choices you can make in your life right now to start taking control of your future.

<u>Can Control</u>   <u>Can't Control</u>

Who I'm friends with

Who I choose to be in a romantic relationship with

Whether I finish school

How I discipline my child

What I expose my child to

Where I live in the future (with parents, alone, with baby's parent)

My career or job

My thoughts and feelings

Other people's behavior

How I eat, exercise, and take care of my body

Who my child plays with

How many children I have

What Really Counts in Life

I look at my mother, who got pregnant when she was a teenager. She didn't have nobody there to help her raise me and my brother. My father left us when I was two and we never really saw him much after that. She had a lot of stress on her raising two kids alone and not being from this country or speaking the language that well. She worked hard in a bakery for long hours, but she never complained or took it out on us. Even though she yelled sometimes, her attitude toward her kids was real loving. And she made us believe that we could be something in life. I don't remember growing up feeling poor or bad because we didn't have a dad around. Mostly I remember feeling really loved. And to me, that's what matters most. Not how much money you have or what kind of house you live in, but getting love and giving it. You don't need money to have patience, love, or kindness. I want my baby to feel that way. I think of those things as my gift to him.

Rosa, 22 years old

Rosa's right. What it takes to raise a healthy, happy baby are the things that don't cost money. What does matter is the love you show him, the patience you treat him with, and the good decisions you make about his physical and emotional safety. Being a great parent is about getting up every single day and trying to raise your child with love and kindness. It means being mature and decent. It means accepting help when you need it.

Raising a child well is the single most important thing you can do in your entire life. It is a gift to your child, your family, and the world. And everything you need to create a positive future for your baby is already in you and in this book. When things get difficult (and they will!), remind yourself that you have the power to be a great parent. So, is there a secret to being a great parent? Something we haven't told you yet? When it comes right down to it, being a great parent is about NEVER GIVING UP. EVER. We wish you the best future possible for you and your child.

Remember:

You have the power to be a great parent!
You are strong.
You are wise.
And most importantly, enjoy your child
each and every day!

Tell Us What You Think

If *Power Source Parenting* helped you or made a difference in your life we'd love to hear about it.

You can write to us at:

**The Lionheart Foundation
Box 194 Back Bay
Boston, MA 02117**

Bibliography

Faber, A., & Mazlish, E. (1980). *How to talk so kids will listen and listen so kids will talk.* New York: Avon Books.

The Healthy Families San Angelo Curriculum. (1992). *Healthy Babies. Healthy Families.* San Angelo, Texas.

Kazdin, A.E. (2005). *Parent management training: Treatment for oppositional, aggressive, and antisocial behavior in children and adolescents.* New York: Oxford University Press.

Levy, B. (1993). *In love and in danger.* Emeryville, CA: Avalon.

Linehan, M.M., (1993). *Skills Training manual for treating borderline personality disorder.* New York: Guilford Press.

Marvin, R., Cooper, G., Hoffman, K., & Powell, B. (2002). The circle of security project: Attachment-based intervention with caregiver-pre-school child dyads. *Attachment and Human Development, 4,* 107-124.

Shelov, S.P., &Hannemann, R.E. (Eds.). (2004). *The American Academy of Pediatrics. The complete and authoritative guide: Caring for your baby and child. Birth to age five.* New York: Bantam Books.

Ordering Information

Power Source Parenting can be ordered through the Lionheart
Foundation.
After the Lionheart Foundation reaches its goal of free distribution to
programs for young parents throughout the United States, if Lionheart
has funds, free copies will be sent to young parents (upon request)
who do not have the means to pay.

Individual copies: $12 plus $3 s&h. Total $15

Bulk rates are available for orders of over nine copies.

For orders outside of the U.S. and Canada, please send only
checks drawn on a U.S. bank in U.S. dollars, or an international postal
money order in U.S. dollars

We accept Visa, Mastercard, or check or money order payable to:

The Lionheart Foundation
Box 194 Back Bay
Boston, MA 02117

www.lionheart.org

Bethany Casarjian, Ph.D., is the Clinical Director of The Lionheart Foundation's National Emotional Literacy Project for Youth At-Risk. She is also the co-author of *Power Source: Taking Charge of Your Life.* Over the past fifteen years Bethany has worked in a variety of settings serving young people facing significant life challenges. Most recently she was the director of the Heritage School's mental health clinic in East Harlem, New York. Bethany also co-created the Treatment for Residents with Incarcerated Parents program (TRIP) at The Children's Village in Dobbs Ferry, NY. In addition, she was an adjunct professor at Teachers College, Columbia University. Her most important job to date, however, has been raising her three children.

Also Available from The Lionheart Foundation

In addition to *Power Source Parenting*, The Lionheart Foundation publishes a book/emotional literacy curriculum for at-risk teens and young adults titled *Power Source: Taking Charge of Your Life* (available in English and Spanish). This program is currently used in more than 2500 schools, institutions, and community programs across the United States. Designed for use with individuals or groups, *Power Source: Taking Charge of Your Life* can be implemented as a core curriculum or as an adjunct to anger management, recovery, or life skills programs. In addition to this book, the *Power Source Facilitator's Manual* and the *Power Source* Video Series are also available. (See www.lionheart.org)

Power Source: Taking Charge of Your Life addresses:

- Techniques and strategies for impulse control, anger management, and conflict resolution
- Identifying ways to recognize and manage high-risk triggers
- Histories of childhood abuse and neglect and the related feelings of shame, grief, anger, and loss
- Victim awareness and taking responsibility for offending behavior
- The development of a cohesive sense of self and a positive future orientation

The Value of Using *Power Source Parenting* and *Power Source* Jointly

One book is incapable of containing all the information and guidance that at-risk youth need to heal and go on to be effective parents. For this reason, we strongly recommend using *Power Source: Taking Charge of Your Life* in conjunction with *Power Source Parenting* to help young parents and their children end intergenerational cycles of high-risk behavior and lead productive lives.